FACE 2 FACE

Elisha

Encountering t… /ation

JIM WINTER

ERIES EDITOR: SIMON J ROBINSON

DayOne

First printed 2008

ISBN 978–1–84625–113–9

British Library Cataloguing in Publication Data available

Published by Day One Publications
Ryelands Road, Leominster, HR6 8NZ
Telephone 01568 613 740 FAX 01568 611 473

email—sales@dayone.co.uk
web site—www.dayone.co.uk

Printed by Gutenberg Press, Malta.

'Called to succeed the great Elijah in ministering to Israel in godless and corrupt times, Elisha faced enormous challenges. Jim Winter brings us face to face with this under-appreciated prophet, reminding us all the while that the God who was sufficient for him is still sufficient. Ministers of the gospel may find special encouragement for their own challenges by walking with Jim Winter in the footprints of the prophet. The many illustrations make Jim Winter's book very readable. The applications make it very helpful. The pictures of Christ make it very valuable, reminding us that in Christ alone we find meaning for this life and hope for the life to come.'

Roger Ellsworth,
Minister of Immanuel Baptist Church, Benton, Illinois

'All credit to Jim Winter for the way he opens up the life of Elisha. He takes us into the past through the pages of Scripture and brings us face to face with this great prophet. Then he brings Elisha into our present, deftly drawing out the principles that make him relevant to our day. But then he goes one step further. With warmth and biblical sensitivity he brings us to Christ. So here, in handling these passages, Jim Winter does what every true expositor should do: he brings us face to face with Jesus!'

Mark G Johnston,
Minister of Grove Chapel, Camberwell, England

Contents

1 Servants of salvation

1 Kings 19:15–21

The weeks leading up to the beginning of another farming year were tough for God's prophet Elijah. His long battle with the weak and wicked King Ahab and his manipulative wife, Jezebel, was not yet finished. His great victory over the prophets and priests of Baal on Mount Carmel had stirred the people to declare, 'The LORD, he is God!' (1 Kings 18:39) and even seemed to bring the king into line, but Jezebel was a tougher nut to crack. She had made it clear to God's prophet that, in her eyes, he was a marked man.

A long journey of forty days brought him to Mount Horeb and to a cave where God prepared him for the calling of three men who would be instrumental in restoring the worship of the one true God in Israel—Hazael, Jehu and Elisha (1 Kings 19:15–17).

In obedience, Elijah made his way northwards to Abel Meholah, passing through the Jordan valley, where the recent rain had softened the parched fields. Everywhere was a hive of activity as farmers prepared their fields for sowing. Shaphat's farm at Abel Meholah lay at the northern end of the Jordan valley, about halfway between the Sea of Galilee and the Dead Sea. It is generally identified today with Tel Abu Sifri. When Solomon divided his kingdom, Abel Meholah provided the border for his fifth district. It had little significance except for being one of the destinations of the fleeing Midian army in the days of Gideon.

People are called to serve God in a number of different ways and from a diversity of backgrounds. David was looking after the sheep when called to his father's house to be anointed king by the prophet Samuel. Peter and John were engaged in a fishing business, preparing for another catch; and Matthew was collecting taxes when called to lay his money on the table and become a disciple of Christ. The evangelist D. L. Moody turned from selling shoes to saving souls. William Booth, the founder of the Salvation Army, was at work in a pawnbroker's, trading on the poverty of his customers, when God called him to a work of taking 'soup, soap and salvation' to the masses of poor throughout the world.

Elisha, the son of Shaphat, was ploughing. It was a busy time on the farm and there was no place for interruption or diversions from the work at hand. There was much to be done—and quickly. Being a wealthy farmer, Shaphat was able to employ twelve yoke of oxen, one driven by Elisha. As the young man was ploughing he was approached by Elijah and felt the prophet's cloak fall upon his shoulders.

How is a person called by God to serve in the cause of his kingdom? Callings occur in different ways and in different situations, but we can learn two important principles when we examine the way in which Elijah was used in the provision of his successor.

GOD ORDAINS THE CIRCUMSTANCES (VV. 15–18)

THE STATE OF THE NATION

Jezebel was fanatically and congenitally opposed to the religion of Israel. Her father, Ethbaal, king of Sidon, had murdered his predecessor and had elevated himself to the position of king as well as chief priest of the goddess Astarte. She married Ahab and systematically set about eliminating the worship of Yahweh in Israel, replacing it with the worship of Baal. She began by removing from her husband's heart any vestige of loyalty to the religion of his forefathers (1 Kings 16:29–33). Urged on by Jezebel, Ahab transferred his allegiance to Baal (21:25). From then on, it became relatively easy for her to widen her sweep of the nation. She hunted down and eliminated the true prophets of Yahweh and packed the royal court with her own men. False prophets still spoke in the name of Yahweh, but had a heart to please only the queen (Jeremiah 23:16–32); others were openly speaking on behalf of Baal, producing and promoting satanic practices in the nation. No wonder the people were confused when challenged regarding their allegiance (18:21)!

Even after Yahweh's great victory at Carmel, Elijah seemed afraid and alone (19:3,10), but behind the scenes God was working to an unseen plan.[1] In fact, Elijah was one among seven thousand who had not forsaken their God (19:18). There was still much work for him to do, but now was the time for him to anoint a successor who would carry on the work and bring it to fruition.

AN OBEDIENT SERVANT

Great servants of God have an eye for the future and are obedient to God when they prepare to step aside from the work to which God called them. When David was refused the privilege of building the temple, he made provision for its structure by preparing the materials for his son Solomon (1 Chronicles 22).

Twenty years before his death, John Wesley became burdened for the future of the Methodist movement that he had largely founded and built. His brother Charles was the natural choice to be his successor but it soon became clear that he would not be suited to the role. William Grimshaw came to mind, but irreconcilable differences soon separated the two men. Later, John Fletcher seemed the ideal candidate, but ill health and a premature death ruled him out. Wesley knew, however, that God would continue the work after he had gone. Hence his famous remark: 'God buries his workmen, but his work goes on.'

It is easy to become so embroiled in our own service that we fail to heed the prompting of God to provide for the time when we are to step aside and hand the work over to another. Churches have been blighted by those who have clung to office or to a specific role long past the period of their usefulness, while there has been someone waiting in the wings who has been prepared by God to take up the work.

Even as he was instructing Elijah on the next part of his mission, God was preparing the three men who would be instrumental in meting out his judgement on Ahab and Jezebel. When we read the history of what happened by the hand of these three men, we can see that Elisha did not literally anoint them with oil, but God was clearly on the case and these 'anointed' or chosen vessels would be his instruments in Ahab and Jezebel's downfall.

Hazael was a high official in the court of Ben-Hadad of Syria. Later he was sent to Elisha when Ben-Hadad was taken ill. The prophet revealed to Hazael the slaughter that would take place among the Israelites under his hand (2 Kings 8:7–15). Hazael returned to the palace, smothered the king, ascended the throne of Syria and became a menace to both Israel and Judah (2 Kings 8:28–30; 10:32; 12:17–18; 13:3–22).

Jehu was a member of Ahab's bodyguard who later ruthlessly set about wiping out the idolatrous practices of the Ahab dynasty. In a systematic purge of the supporters of Baal, he assassinated Ahab's son, Jehoram (Joram); Ahaziah, king of Judah; and Jezebel (2 Kings 9–10).

Elisha, however, was supremely the one chosen to bring justice and righteousness back to the nation of Israel. His name meant 'God is salvation', and, as his story unfolds, we shall see that he certainly lived up to that name! His nature and style of ministry were in marked contrast to those of Elijah. Whereas Elijah was essentially a 'loner', Elisha was an outgoing character who ministered happily with others, founding his own prophetic communities. Here indeed was a worthy successor to the great prophet. God uses all kinds of people for the work of his kingdom!

GOD ORDAINS THE PERSON (VV. 19–21)

THE CALL TO SERVE (V. 19)

Not a word was said at this point between Elijah and Elisha. It seems that Elijah simply placed his cloak over Elisha's shoulders and walked on. But Elisha seemed to sense the significance of what was happening. As Matthew Henry put it, 'An invisible hand touched his heart, and unaccountably inclined him by a secret power, without any external persuasions, to quit his husbandry and give himself to the ministry.'[2]

Towards the end of the 1930s, Dr Campbell Morgan, the eminent minister of Westminster Chapel, London, was looking for an associate minister who would eventually succeed him. Dr Martyn Lloyd-Jones, whose powerful preaching ministry in Aberavon, South Wales, had become widely known, was linked with the post. Although Lloyd-Jones had preached at Westminster Chapel, he dismissed any idea that he would play a significant role in that particular church in the near future. While preaching in Philadelphia, USA, in 1937, Lloyd-Jones noticed Campbell Morgan in the congregation. Morgan greeted Lloyd-Jones at the end of the service and slowly walked away. As Lloyd-Jones talked with others he could not fail to notice the elderly preacher intermittently pause, turn and look back at him as he slowly made his way up the aisle. Within two years he had become Morgan's associate minister, and on Morgan's retirement in 1943, he embarked on an illustrious ministry in the heart of London that would continue for the next twenty-five years.

THE CALL TO DISCIPLESHIP (VV. 20–21)

'[Elisha] left the oxen and ran after Elijah … Then he arose and followed Elijah, and became his servant.' It was as if Elisha had been prepared by God for this moment. He was already exhibiting the attitude of one who was willing to serve in whatever situation God placed him in. Although he was the son of a wealthy farmer, it was not beneath him to share the toil and sweat of a hard day's work among the other labourers on his father's farm. For the godly man or woman, every act of service is for God's glory (1 Corinthians 10:31), and every act of obedience, however small, is noted by the Lord (Luke 16:10–12).

Elisha was willing to give up the comfort of Abel Meholah and follow Elijah into an unknown future. He was prepared to forsake the status and privilege of his current position to become nothing more than a servant—even taking on the task of washing his master's hands (2 Kings 3:11).

PREPARATION FOR SERVICE (V. 20)

Elisha's only plea to the prophet was, 'Let me kiss my father and mother goodbye.' It is useful to contrast his request with the story of a man who had a similar encounter with Jesus (Luke 9:61–62). Jesus' words to him appear to challenge or belittle Elisha's desire to say goodbye to his parents: 'No one, having put his hand to the plow, and looking back, is fit for the kingdom of God' (Luke 9:62). But the circumstances were very different. This man was prevaricating in his commitment, as revealed by his words: 'Lord, I will follow you, but …'! He still appeared to be hankering after the security of his home and family. In Elisha's case there was a desire to take this action as an act of consecration to his new calling. As Dale Ralph Davis puts it, 'Elisha goes back to *sever* his connections, not to delay his commitment.'[3] Elisha's next actions in the matter leave the reader in no doubt as to this (1 Kings 19:21)!

Elijah's reply was a little ambiguous: 'Go back again, for what have I done to you?' It certainly does not mean that Elijah felt that he had made a mistake in calling Elisha, nor that he sensed Elisha's desire to be an act of disobedience or rejection. Here was Elisha's first test. Surrounded by those he loved, in the security of his family home, with the emotional pull to stay and the stark realization of what he was about to do in leaving all this behind, he had to keep in mind the magnitude of his calling. It is easy to say 'Yes' in principle, but the time comes when the emotional cost must be counted.

CONSECRATION TO SERVICE (V. 21)

Elisha's actions were swift and decisive. Everything that denoted his position on the farm was destroyed, not in a frenzied desire to remove the temptation to change his mind, but rather as an act of consecration and celebration of his call to a new and wider field of service. Plough and oxen—his former means of employment—were sacrificed in a celebratory meal for family and workers.

Many tears would have been shed. Shaphat and his family would miss the faithful Elisha, but they were godly people and willingly accepted this call of their son. There would be times when Shaphat, like the father of the prodigal (Luke 15), would be tempted to scan the horizon for his returning son. This son, however, was not lost in a far country. Shaphat had named him at birth 'God is salvation', and he would now carry that message of salvation to the people of Israel.

The time had come for Elisha to turn his back upon Abel Meholah and follow Elijah.

For further study ▶

FOR FURTHER STUDY

1. *What are the similarities and differences between Elisha's call and those of David (1 Samuel 16:1–13), Peter (Mark 1:14–20; Luke 5:1–12) and Paul (Acts 9:1–19)?*
2. *Elisha was a 'messenger of salvation' to Israel, yet God also used Hazael and Jehu to bring righteousness to his people. How does God's mercy equate with his judgement? (See John 12:37–50; Romans 2:1–16; 3:21–26.)*

FOR FURTHER STUDY

1. *How does the obedience of Elijah and Elisha compare with that in your own life and experience?*
2. *What principles can be found in this passage that help the individual, the local church and Christian organizations in determining a person's call to service?*
3. *How sensitive would you be to God's call if his cloak were placed around your shoulders?*

Notes

1. See **Simon J. Robinson,** *Face2Face with Elijah* (Leominster: Day One Publications, 2007).
2. **Matthew Henry,** *Commentary on the Whole Bible*, (London: Pickering and Inglis, n. d.), vol. 2, p. 685.
3. **Dale Ralph Davis,** *The Wisdom and the Folly*, (Fearn, Tain: Christian Focus Publications, 2005), p. 281.

2 The cloak of office

2 Kings 2:1–18

Little is known of the time Elisha and Elijah spent together before Elijah was taken up into heaven on a whirlwind. This period, however, saw the unfolding of God's judgement on the house of Ahab. After defeating the armies of Ben-Hadad, Israel experienced a short time of peace. Then Ahab and Jehoshaphat, king of Judah, made an alliance to attack Ramoth Gilead. As the battle proceeded Ahab was killed and his body was taken back to Samaria and buried. Ahab was gone, but his dynasty was still intact and fervent in its opposition to the true God of Israel.

For the next two years Ahaziah reigned over Israel, continuing in the evil ways of his father, while Jezebel lurked menacingly in the background. Injured by a fall from a window, Ahaziah consulted the Baalite prophets of his parents and Elijah was sent by God to prophesy his death, demonstrating his God-given authority by summoning fire from heaven that consumed two captains and 100 men from the palace guard! The heirless king was succeeded by his brother Jehoram (Joram).

Accompanying Elijah on his final journey, Elisha prepared for the time when he would be left alone to continue and extend the work of Elijah. This period reveals much about the kind of life he was to lead as the major spokesman for Yahweh for the next fifty years.

A LIFE OF FELLOWSHIP (VV. 1–6)

LOYALTY (VV. 1–2)

God meets with and ministers to his people in many ways. We must learn never to expect him to conform to any pattern. The God who spoke to Elijah in the 'still small voice' at Horeb was going to transport him to heaven in glorious splendour!

Why did Elijah not want Elisha with him as he prepared for his final journey (v. 2)? Some have suggested that this was out of humility—he did not want anyone to witness the glory he was about to experience. But we do not know the extent of Elijah's foreknowledge of the amazing event that was about to take place. It may have been a test of Elisha's fidelity and love. Or it simply may have been that Elijah, ignorant of Elisha's own foreknowledge of the event, was unsure as to God's will at that point.

Nevertheless, Elijah seemed almost relieved that Elisha still wanted to be with him. This conversation would be repeated twice more before Elijah was taken up into heaven. There is a parallel to this in Jesus' three questions to Peter: 'Do you love me?' (John 21:15–19).

It is important to note Elisha's personal loyalty to Elijah and its place in God's plan. This may well have clouded the hearts and minds of the disciples of Jesus as his own death drew near. They too were about to lose a friend! But the overruling factor was Elisha's loyalty to God. The true prophet or servant of God is aware that he is only a very small part in a greater plan that involves the lives and ministries of others. Loyalty to God involves loyalty to God's servants. Whatever his other personality traits may have been, Elisha was not a 'loner'. It was God's will and God's glory that was pre-eminent in his mind.

Elisha knew he was the 'prophet in waiting' but he remained steadfastly devoted to the present incumbent until such time as God decided for the transition to take place. There was no evidence of the frustration or impatience of a politician eager for the departure of the party leader so that he or she can become number one, or of the successor to a throne waiting for the ageing monarch to die so a new reign can begin.

APPREHENSION (VV. 3–6)

As we have already observed, Elijah trod carefully in his desire to know God's will as to when he must take leave of Elisha. There was a kind of transition in their relationship at this point, for the great prophet was willing to accept Elisha's insistence as a word from God himself. Here was true humility.

The prophets from Bethel and Jericho challenged Elisha with the same question: 'Do you know that the LORD will take away your master from over you today?' (vv. 3,5). Their motive for approaching Elisha in this way is unclear. They may simply have been unsure as to whether he knew this—or they may have been eager to show that they too had been entrusted with knowledge of this great event. It is unlikely that, as some have suggested, they wished to hurt Elisha with the news of his impending loss. But one thing is clear: Elisha was stung by their question!

His response was emphatic: 'Yes, I know; keep silent!' Again, we must search for a reason for his reply. Some have suggested that he did not want the event to become common knowledge, turning an intimate revelation of glory into a mere circus! Others point to Elijah's humility in not wanting his moment of beatification witnessed by others. A simpler explanation would be that Elisha wanted them to ponder the solemnity of the event. Like the disciples of Jesus, he was, even now, experiencing the pangs of bereavement. Fully aware that his master was to be taken from him, he rejected every reminder of the moment when he would be left alone. Such events are filled with apprehension for those who are left behind.

A LIFE OF INTIMACY WITH GOD (VV. 7–10)

The fifty prophets accompanied Elijah and Elisha to the banks of the Jordan to become eyewitnesses from a distance of the glory that would unfold before them. In a manner reminiscent of Moses striking the Red Sea with his shepherd's crook, the symbol of his office, Elijah rolled up his cloak and struck the Jordan, parting the water and enabling the two men to cross over on dry land.

After they had crossed the river, Elijah granted Elisha one final request: 'Ask! What may I do for you, before I am taken away from you?' There have been a number of interpretations of Elisha's reply: 'Please let a double portion of your spirit be upon me' (v. 9).

It appears that Elisha was seeking some kind of verification of his ministry to stand him in good stead among the other prophets after Elijah had been taken from them. Most commentators agree that Elisha was asking in accordance with the law that the firstborn must receive double the inheritance of the other sons (Deuteronomy 21:17). This would establish Elisha's right as 'the firstborn son' of Elijah. He was not seeking greater gifts but simply recognized his own inadequacy; without the Holy Spirit we are powerless!

Elijah knew that he did not have the power to grant Elisha's request. He had God's anointing, and only God could anoint his successor. His reply was a test of God's will in the matter (v. 10).

A LIFE OF GRACE AND GLORY (VV. 11–12)

The ascension of Elijah has been compared with that of Enoch (Genesis 5:24; Hebrews 11:5). It has also been likened to that of Moses (Deuteronomy 32:48–52; 34:5–6), especially given his appearance with Elijah on the Mount of Transfiguration (Matthew 17:3). There was a marked difference, however, between the earthly departure of the two men: the body of Moses was buried by God, but Elijah's body was taken into heaven. Elijah's ascension is also portrayed as a forerunner of that of Christ himself (Acts 1:9), and also as a prophetic picture of the visible rapture of the church (1 Thessalonians 4:17).

However well prepared we are, God's moment is both sudden and unexpected. On the day of Pentecost, Christ's disciples were meeting together. We are not told what they were doing, but we are told that 'suddenly there came a sound from heaven, as of a rushing mighty wind, and it filled the whole house' (Acts 2:2). Elijah and Elisha were walking along together and talking together. Maybe there were final instructions to be given—words of advice and encouragement—for there was still work to be done. These were not men who were just sitting and waiting for something to happen. As Matthew Henry put it, 'We mistake if we think our preparation for heaven is carried on only by contemplation and acts of devotion.'[1]

George Whitefield laboured long and hard in the cause of his Saviour. The day before he died, sick and exhausted, he delivered a two-hour sermon to a congregation earnestly seeking a word from God. Arnold Dallimore's account of his final hours, spent in the home of a fellow minister, reveals the spirit of a man who will labour on until God calls him home: 'While the family was at supper he said he was tired and would go to bed. He had reached the landing stairs when the door was opened to admit a host who had gathered outside, who most earnestly requested that he preach to them. He paused, candle in hand, and preached Christ, till the candle burned out in its socket and died away. That candle was symbolic of his life, also burned out and speedily dying away.'[2]

For Elisha—the messenger of salvation—the scene was full of images of that salvation in action. Here were symbols of God's authority and conquest, 'the chariot of Israel and its horsemen', clothed in his awesome purifying fire. His faithful servant was carried safely home by the storm-wind of God's judgement (Isaiah 25:4). God will judge all men with justice (Acts 17:31), but, for his redeemed people, Christ has received that judgement upon himself (2 Corinthians 5:21) and has gone into heaven to prepare a place for them; one day he will come again to receive them to himself (John 14:3).

Awestruck by the scene that unfolded before him, Elisha tore his clothes as a sign of his bereavement. This also enabled him to put on Elijah's cloak of office. Likewise, Christians throw off the filthy rags of their own righteousness and put on the salvation garment of Christ.

A LIFE OF POWER (VV. 13–14)

Elijah's cloak had fallen from him as he ascended into heaven. Elisha picked it up and advanced to the river that the two men had recently crossed. Striking the water with it, he cried, 'Where is the LORD God of Elijah?' (v. 14). This was not the desperate cry of someone who doubted God's presence, but a loud affirmation of faith in the God who had empowered the man that he had served and had now succeeded. Too often, God's people look to men and not to the God who had mightily used them. We rightly celebrate the lives and revere the memory of those who have been instrumental in times of revival, but we forget that their God is our God and that he has not changed.

Elisha's cry drew a rapid response from heaven. 'Then he took the mantle of Elijah that had fallen from him, and struck the water' (v. 14). The river divided and he crossed over. The spirit of Elijah now rested on Elisha. Or, more accurately, God, who had set aside Elijah and empowered him, had now confirmed the succession of that work in another. Is it insignificant that Elisha's first miracle should mirror Elijah's last?

A LIFE OF RESPONSIBILITY (VV. 15–18)

It is difficult to ascertain how much of the whole scene had been witnessed by the prophets from Jericho. It is clear, however, that they saw the waters part as Elisha struck them with his cloak, and that this action confirmed to them Elisha's succession and also accredited him as the new leader of the prophets in Israel. Cloaked with his new responsibilities, Elisha was thrust into making his first decision. His response revealed what kind of leader he was going to be.

A leader has to accept that those who follow will only have partial vision and understanding. It is how he deals with this that shows his true merit. Elisha was perfectly clear in his own mind as to what God had done in taking Elijah into heaven. Yet the prophets had only watched from afar and placed their own limited interpretation on what had actually happened. They had recognized the power of God but did not understand the way in which God had exercised this power. They firmly believed that the Spirit of the Lord had taken Elijah—but where and how? Some may have thought that God had simply taken him to another part of the country for other work—as happened later in the case of Philip and the Ethiopian (Acts 8:39). Some may have believed that, as in the case of Moses, God had taken his spirit and left his body behind. Like the women who came to the tomb of Jesus, they wanted to honour the body of the one whom they loved (Mark 16:1–3).

At first, Elisha refused, but the prophets persisted in their request. A leader has, at times, to pause and let those who follow catch up with him. Elisha was obviously disappointed that he had not been able to convince them through his own authority and he saw the need to let them find out for themselves. Returning to Jericho, he left them to engage in their fruitless task. On their return, he did not rebuke them but simply responded, 'Did I not say to you, "Do not go"?' His wisdom and authority were now firmly established and it was time to move on to the work to which God had called him.

FOR FURTHER STUDY

1. *Note how Jesus taught his disciples to follow his example and serve one another (Matthew 20:27; 23:11) and how Paul concurred (Galatians 5:13; Philippians 2:5–11).*

2. *Compare the ways in which God called the following people to serve him: Moses (Exodus 3), Isaiah (Isaiah 6), Peter (Matthew 4:18–22; 16:13–20), Paul (Acts 9:1–19; 22:1–21), and David (1 Samuel 16). What are the common features?*

FOR FURTHER STUDY

1. *What are the most important qualities to look for in a Christian leader?*

2. *How can the Christian leader best exercise his authority in the church? See 1 Peter 5:1–5 and 2 Corinthians 11:1–15.*

Notes

1. **Henry,** *Commentary*, vol. 2, p. 714.
2. **Arnold Dallimore,** *George Whitefield* (London: The Wakeman Trust, 1990), p. 215.

3 A tale of two cities

2 Kings 2:19–25

This passage records the power of God exercised through his servant in both salvation and judgement. It also prefigures the mercy of God and the judgement of God in the ministry of the Lord Jesus Christ.

THE CURE IN A CURSED CITY (VV. 19–22)

JERICHO—A CITY UNDER A CURSE

Jericho was known as the 'city of palms' (Deuteronomy 34:3). It was the first city to oppose the Israelites as they crossed over into Canaan during the time of Joshua and it was razed to the ground (Joshua 6). God placed a curse on anyone who tried to rebuild it (Joshua 6:26). It was also the site of the first recorded sin committed in the promised land, through Achan's greed (Joshua 7). During the reign of Ahab, the city was rebuilt by Hiel of Bethel, who soon experienced the effect of that curse in the death of his two sons (1 Kings 16:34). The new Jericho soon became a flourishing city, but the curse remained and soon manifested itself in another form by the time the newly ordained prophet Elisha arrived.

THE ACTIONS OF THE PROPHET

Elisha's actions were similar to the miracle performed by Jesus at Cana in Galilee (John 2:1–11), where he turned the water into wine. Elisha was specific with his instructions to the servants. Under God's hand he knew exactly what to do.

THE SALT

In Old Testament times salt was used in a number of ways. Its qualities meant that it could be used primarily as a cleansing agent and preservative. Meat and fish packed in salt would be preserved for times when there was little or no fresh food. Salt was also used as part of the temple ritual. The cereal offerings were seasoned with salt to typify the eternal nature of God's covenant with Israel (Leviticus 2:13). The salt, however, had to be pure. Even the vessel used was not to pollute it! Most of the salt available to Israel would have been rock salt gathered from the Dead Sea area. The pure salt lay beneath the outer layer which was adulterated by other elements, thus rendering it tasteless and ineffective. This was sometimes sold cheaply. Jesus referred to it in the Sermon on the Mount as a salt that 'loses its flavour' (Matthew 5:13).

THE WATER

The casting of the salt into the water had an immediate effect, which was not, however, merely a chemical one. The salt would certainly not have made the water pure for drinking purposes, and the flooding of the land with salt water would have had a disastrous effect on the vegetation. The salt was rather a symbol of God's supernatural power in rendering the water pure and productive. Elisha gave God the credit for this:

'Thus says the LORD: "I have healed this water; from it there shall be no more death or barrenness"' (v. 21). The effect was long term, for the water 'remains healed to this day'.

THE MERCY OF GOD IN THE MINISTRY OF CHRIST

The casting of the salt into the spring had a prophetic significance. It demonstrated that God was going to purify the polluted condition of men's hearts and lives through the use of a clean vessel and the casting of a common, yet pure, substance into that condition. Christ, the Son of God, entered the cesspool of our fallen humanity in his pure humanity in order to bring about the cleansing of our lives.

We can easily see the parallels between this event and one of the ways in which Jesus described his own ministry. When he met with a woman at the well at Sychar, he told her of water that would permanently satisfy a person's thirst. When he saw the woman's bemusement, he responded by telling her that 'Whoever drinks of this water [from the well] will thirst again, but whoever drinks of the water that I shall give him will never thirst ... [It] will become in him a fountain of water springing up into everlasting life' (John 4:13–14).

Just as the city of Jericho lay under a curse, so man, in sin, is under the curse of the law (Galatians 3:10). Christ's death upon the cross was like God's salt thrown into the polluted waters, removing the curse for eternity, so that by faith in him, 'Christ has redeemed us from the curse of the law, having become a curse for us' (Galatians 3:13).

THE CURSE IN THE 'HOUSE OF GOD' (VV. 23–25)

In the midst of the great work that Elisha had been given in

God's plan for the salvation of his people, we have an incident that troubles and perplexes many who read it. Here is a man who has been empowered to purify the water supply of a city, and even raise the dead, overreacting in a seemingly malicious and vindictive way to the jibes of a group of children. However, we need to look closely at the incident before we pass any kind of judgement on God's prophet. When we look at the background to the event, and at the event itself, we discover that this is not the story of a group of children being maliciously destroyed for taunting a bald-headed preacher. It is, as Alfred Edersheim puts it, one of 'Contempt and ridicule of God's servant [and] blasphemy and denial of God's work.'[1]

THE BACKGROUND

A simple act of petulance, even under the severest pressure, was not consistent with Elisha's nature. His very name, 'God is salvation', became the hallmark of his ministry and character. Although he would not withhold a message of judgement from God, he was sent to demonstrate and declare salvation to the people of Israel.

We must not overlook the importance of the place where this event occurred. Bethel, the 'house of God', was one of the most sacred spots in Israel, with historic connections to Abraham and Jacob. By the time of Jeroboam, however, it had become the centre of calf worship. The prophet Hosea called it Beth Aven, the 'house of wickedness' (Hosea 10:5). Elisha had arrived at a place that characterized the wickedness of Israel. All the holy associations of past times had been removed, and what had replaced them now stood as an affront to the prophet.

Out of this city came the young people who now mocked God's prophet Elisha. The Hebrew word that describes them has been translated in a number of ways: 'youths' (NKJV and NIV), 'little children' (AV) and 'small boys' (ESV). In order to establish an age for these young people we must look at the ways in which the Hebrew word is used. It is a masculine noun that can, however, be used to refer to either sex. In the Bible, it has been used to describe a newborn baby in the case of Moses (Exodus 2:8), but also a young man capable of rape (Genesis 34:19)! Dale Ralph Davis refers to these youths as 'young lads' and places their ages at between ten and twelve years old.

THE EVENT

Whatever their age, these young people encounter Elisha as he enters the town. It would seem from the context that this was a deliberate act on their part and not just an accidental meeting, for what they have to say to the prophet is targeted blasphemy rather than youthful derision.

'Go up' is clearly a reference to Elijah's translation to heaven. Here is a statement of mocking disbelief towards this great act of God—a denial of God's sovereignty and power. Their confidence would have been fuelled by the general contempt that the citizens of Bethel had towards the God of Israel. Later in Israel's history, the one who was more than just a messenger of salvation also heard such a cry, a mocking of the God who had come to seek and save the lost (Matthew 27:41–43).

Although, like most travellers, Elisha would almost certainly have had his head covered, the cry went out, 'You baldhead!' Elisha had been deliberately targeted for this abuse.

This was a term of great contempt (premature baldness was often associated with leprosy) and we do not even know if Elisha *was* bald!

God's servants can shrug off personal abuse however hurtful it may be. They are called by God to die to self and live for him. But in this case, the glory and honour of God was at stake. It was not the prophet who was being treated with contempt but the God who had sent him to the town. As Mathew Henry put it, 'Mocking the messengers of the Lord, and misusing the prophets, was one of the crying sins of Israel.'[2]

THE JUDGEMENT

The whole future of Elisha's ministry was now on the line. One can almost feel the tugging at his heart strings as he calls down a curse from God upon the young people who are mocking him. 'His authority in Israel was at stake, and with it the results of his prophetic mission. His rising feelings of compassion and love must, therefore, here be sacrificed to the honour and cause of Jehovah, the true God of Bethel and of Israel.'[3]

The bears were a direct judgement from God. We do not know the size of the mob surrounding God's prophet but forty-two of them perished under the claws of these great beasts. God cannot be mocked. A man reaps what he sows (Galatians 6:7). As in the case of Ananias and Sapphira (Acts 5:1–11), we see the folly of those who make light of God's promises of judgement on those who reject him.

We do not know the mind of Elisha as he retired to Mount Carmel and journeyed to Samaria. But his evangelical nature suggests to us that he must have been deeply saddened by the events of that day. Alfred Edersheim puts it well: 'Surely on the evening of that day of judgement, there was not a sadder heart even in Bethel than that of the lonely pilgrim to Carmel.'[4]

THE JUDGEMENT OF GOD IN THE MINISTRY OF CHRIST

Just as it was folly for these youths to mock the messenger of salvation, so it is equally foolish and dangerous today to overlook the Bible passages that refer to Jesus Christ as the judge of all men. Those who reject him will one day cry to the rocks and mountains to fall on them, to hide them from the wrath of the Lamb (Revelation 6:16). Like Elisha, Christ longs that men and women will repent and turn to God and receive the salvation freely given to those who do so. He longs to gather his people under his wings and protect them from the judgement (Matthew 23:37–39), but that judgement will surely come, and it is just and righteous (John 5:24–30).

One rainy day does not spoil a summer. Elisha's ministry is fundamentally one of mercy and salvation. God's grace extends itself beyond anything we can imagine—to those who are under the curse of the law (Galatians 3:13). We must remember, however, that he is a God who will judge all who mock him and reject his gracious offer of forgiveness.

For further study ▶

FOR FURTHER STUDY

1. *Study the way in which the Bible describes the consequences of sin as a 'curse' in the following passages: Deuteronomy 11:26–32; 21:22–23; Malachi 2:2; Matthew 25:41; Galatians 3:10–14; Revelation 22:1–5.*

2. *What do the following passages tell us about God's glory: Exodus 3:1–6; 2 Samuel 6:1–9; Isaiah 6:1–8; Jude 24–25?*

FOR FURTHER STUDY

1. *How would you answer someone who complained that Elisha's action was vindictive?*

2. *How would you explain to a person who is not a Christian that 'Christ has redeemed us from the curse of the law'?*

Notes

1. **Alfred Edersheim,** *Practical Truths from Elisha* (Grand Rapids: Kregel Publications, 1982), p. 53.
2. **Henry,** *Commentary*, vol. 2, p. 718.
3. **F. W. Krummacher,** *Elisha: A Prophet for Our Times*, (Grand Rapids: Kregel Publications, 1993), p. 25.
4. **Edersheim,** *Practical Truths*, p. 59.

4 Three kings

2 Kings 3:1–27

During the English Civil War of the seventeenth century, Oliver Cromwell instructed his troops to 'Trust in God and keep your powder dry'. Here were the two essential provisions for the battles that would be fought and won: faith in a sovereign protector, and prudence in preparation and provision for the battle. The three kings who set out to do battle with the Moabites—Jehoram, Jehoshaphat and the king of Edom—had no such faith and made no such provision, but were brought face to face with the reality of God's presence through the prophet Elisha.

A little information as to the place of their kingdoms in the history of God's people helps us understand more fully the meaning of the passage.

AN UNLIKELY ALLIANCE

THE MOABITES

The Moabites had an uneasy peace with Israel, the price being 100,000 lambs and the wool of 100,000 rams (v. 4). After Ahab's death the Moabite king, Mesha, rebelled against Israel.

The Moabites, who occupied the land east of the Dead Sea, were the descendants of Moab, the son of Lot and one of his daughters (Genesis 19:37). They had a chequered relationship with Israel. They had been hostile during the desert wanderings, but Moses was forbidden to attack them (Deuteronomy 2:9), although later God excluded them from the nation of Israel (Deuteronomy 23:3–6). Balak, a Moabite king, called the prophet Balaam to curse Israel (Numbers 22:1–6). Moabite women seduced Israelite soldiers and introduced them to idolatrous practices (Numbers 25).

During the time of the judges, Eglon, the king of Moab, oppressed Israel, occupying Jericho for eighteen years until he was struck down by Ehud. After this, Moab was subject to Israel for eighty years (Judges 3). During the same period there was a famine in Bethlehem; Elimelech, Naomi and their two sons moved to Moab. After Elimelech's death the two sons married Moabite women, one being Ruth, the ancestor of Jesus Christ.

Saul warred with Moab (1 Samuel 14:47), but David left his parents under the protection of the king of Moab (1 Samuel 22:1–4). Later, the Moabites became subject to David (2 Samuel 8:2). After Solomon's death, the Moabites broke free, but were subdued by Omri, king of Israel, and remained so until Ahab's death.

THE EDOMITES

The Edomites, who were descendants of Esau, occupied the area to the south of the Dead Sea. Their history runs parallel to that of Moab. Jehoshaphat, king of Judah, had great trouble with them. Along with the Moabites and the Ammonites they had attacked Judah, but in the end started fighting one another. Jehoshaphat eventually subdued them and placed a deputy in place as their king (1 Kings 22:47; 2 Chronicles 20:1).

Here, then, is the background to the events recorded in this chapter. We can learn much by observing the behaviour of these kings.

THE FAILURE OF COMPROMISE (VV. 1–3)

Some people want to have a relationship with God but do not want it on his terms. Consequently, they seek alternative routes that appeal to man's fallen nature. In these verses we can see three of these routes.

RIGHTEOUSNESS BY ASSOCIATION (V. 1)

I once heard a psychiatrist say, 'Always remember that nothing is as good as it seems, and nothing is as bad as it seems.' Although this dictum cannot be applied to the nature of God and the way in which he operates in the life of the Christian, it is often found to be true when we are assessing the motives and behaviour of our fellow human beings. How often have we been thrilled when a public figure has professed faith in Jesus Christ, only to have been disappointed when that person has abandoned his or her new faith or, at best, been seen publicly to compromise it by certain behaviour! It seems that in so many cases there is only partial restoration. There are some who believe that, by associating with good people, they will in some way reflect something of that goodness in their own lives.

When Jehoram succeeded Ahab as king of Israel, Jehoshaphat had been on the throne of Judah for seventeen years. By linking with Jehoshaphat, Jehoram may well have been thinking that somehow he was going to have the assurance of God's blessing and protection on his own life (vv. 6–7). Later, he was severely wounded in a campaign against Syria (8:28–29) and was assassinated by Jehu while convalescing with his mother, Jezebel, at Jezreel. His body was thrown into Naboth's vineyard (9:14–37).

RIGHTEOUSNESS BY DEGREE (V. 2)

When it came to doing evil, Jehoram was not in the same league as Ahab and Jezebel. He had the courage to demolish the sacred stone of Baal that his father had erected—even though his mother was still alive—but he did not take the reforms far enough and rid the land of its idolatry. He, like many before him and since, saw fit to tackle what he considered to be the greater evils, while happily co-existing with other evils. We can easily be deceived into applying this principle to our own lives. Sins do not fall into categories or have tables of importance; all sin separates us from God.

HALF RIGHTEOUSNESS IS BETTER THAN NONE (V. 3)

Like Jehoram, we can accommodate 'acceptable' sins as if they were of no consequence to our relationship with God. We can go for a kind of partial deliverance. Some people do this by differentiating between the work of Christ in their lives as Saviour and that as Lord. As Saviour, he has purchased salvation and assured the believer of a place in heaven; as Lord, he has complete dominion over the Christian's life. There are some who erroneously believe that Christ can be their Saviour and that they can still retain lordship over their own lives. The Bible speaks of no such division.

MAN'S EXTREMITY—GOD'S OPPORTUNITY (VV. 4–20)

OUR BEST PLANS CAN FAIL (VV. 4–9)

Here is a strong alliance of kings and nations. Jehoram and Jehoshaphat mobilized and combined their armies in order to put the king of Moab—who had rebelled against Israel's rule—in his place. They were clear in the route that was going to take them to the place of attack and as they entered the Desert of Edom they were joined by the king of Edom. Everything seemed in place to quell the rebellion and restore the status quo. After seven days, however, it became clear that the plan had a serious flaw—there was no water!

IN TIMES OF ADVERSITY PEOPLE SEEK GOD (VV. 10–12)

Two of these kings had been raised to know the God who brought his people into being. Both Israel and Judah had a great heritage. It was now that they decided to consult their God. If they had consulted him and honoured him in the first place they would not have been in this situation. Their method was to seek him through his prophet, the proven method of the day. How often have we set out on something of our own accord and only brought God into the situation when we have run into trouble?

AN OPPORTUNITY TO EXALT THE LORD (VV. 13–19)

The immediate response of Elisha to the monarchical delegation that stood before him was to refer them to their own gods. The Edomites had their gods, and even though Jehoram had made some inroads into the destruction of the Baalite sites in Israel, he had not completely overthrown the idolatry of his parents. Jehoram, however, believed that it was the true God of Israel that had brought the kings together for judgement, and that only he could save them.

However, one of the party did have the respect of the man of God, and that was Jehoshaphat. For the sake of this one man, the prophet of God was prepared to deliver the other two from inevitable defeat! The presence of a godly man or woman blesses even those who have rejected God. One immediately thinks of Abraham in his plea for the doomed city of Sodom (Genesis 18:16–33). Paul writes of the unbelieving husband being sanctified through his wife, and of the unbelieving wife being sanctified through her believing husband (1 Corinthians 7:14). In other words, the unbelieving spouse is continually under the influence of the godly partner and party to the blessings that the godly partner brings to the relationship. The power of the gospel is ever present in the home and, in due time, that same power may bring the partner to Christ.

Calmed by the playing of a harpist, Elisha delivered God's message to the kings. The message was typical of God. The immediate need was for water, but God was going to do more than they could ask or think (Ephesians 3:20). Water would be provided in abundance and in an overtly miraculous manner. The battle with the Moabites would also result in victory. God was in control of everything! Isn't this so often the case for us, when we set out on some major project, only to be confounded by a specific issue? It is when we turn to the Lord that we find that the whole project is in his care.

THE LORD OUR PROVIDER (V. 20)

When God speaks, he fulfils his spoken word. Jesus said, 'I am the light of the world', and immediately made a blind man see (John 9:1–12). He also said, 'I am the resurrection and the life', and then he raised Lazarus from the dead (John 11:25–44). The very next morning after Elisha had spoken, water flowed from the land of Edom.

JUMPING TO THE WRONG CONCLUSIONS (VV. 21–27)

One of the devices used by writers of soap operas and dramas is to get their characters to jump to wrong conclusions. A snippet from an overheard conversation, or the sighting of a spouse or friend in an apparently compromising but actually perfectly innocent situation, will provide dramatic content for many future episodes!

In fiction, it is merely a device, but in fact, it can lead to disaster—and this was certainly the case for the Moabites. They were well prepared to repel the invading forces of Israel, Judah and Edom, stationing themselves on the border with Edom. As they gazed into the desert looking for evidence of military activity, they were stunned by what lay before them. The once-dry rivers were now awash, not with water but with blood—or at least what appeared to be blood. In fact, the morning sun's reflection had reddened the waters, already stained by the red earth of Edom. Without further investigation or consideration the Moabites quickly reached a fatal conclusion. The armies of Israel and Judah, with their track records of disharmony and animosity, had turned on each other; and the Edomites, long enemies of both kingdoms, had heartily joined in the fray. The 'blood' flowing through the gullies was a signal not to defend but to attack!

Jumping to the wrong conclusion had the direst

consequences for the Moabites. What God had prophesied through Elisha came to pass. Not only did the water that God provided bring blessing to the allies, it was also the means by which the Moabites were brought to destruction.

At the end of the battle, a remarkable event took place in the form of a sacrificial offering of the king of Moab's eldest son. Clear interpretation is difficult. Was the son sacrificed to the Moabite gods or was his death intended to appease Israel? Was the 'indignation against Israel' (v. 27) a Moabite reaction or were the Israelites so shocked by this action that they withdrew? Whatever our understanding of the event, the result was clear—the battle was over for the time being.

What a contrast this is to the offering of God's only Son, the Lord Jesus Christ, not as a last-ditch effort to appease his enemies and obtain temporary relief, but as a sin offering, once for all, planned before the foundation of the world!

For further study ▶

FOR FURTHER STUDY

1. *What do the following passages teach us about God's attitude to compromise: Matthew 6:24; 7:21–23; Luke 18:18–23; Revelation 2:1–7; 2:12–17?*

2. *Note the different ways, both natural and supernatural, in which God delivered his people in the Bible. How many examples can you find? How does he deliver his people today?*

FOR FURTHER STUDY

1. *Can a man or woman know Jesus Christ as his or her Saviour, but not acknowledge him as Lord? Give reasons for your answer.*

2. *How can we best glorify God in our trials? See James 1:3–4; 1 Peter 3:18–4:19.*

5 The oil of joy for mourning

2 Kings 4:1–37

George Müller was a man of faith. Convinced that God had called him into the Christian ministry—and later to found an orphanage—he decided that he would rely solely on God's provision for his needs. Instead of making appeals for money he would leave the matter of how his needs would be met to God alone. His journal records times of great need and then the amazing way in which God spoke to the hearts of others as he met those needs.

GOD'S SERVANTS IN NEED (V. 1)

To serve God does not mean that we will never be in need. There are often times of great testing, when it would appear that our situation is hopeless—but God will never let us down. The apostle Paul found this to be true throughout his arduous and dangerous mission to the Roman world of his day. Later, he wrote to the church at Philippi, 'And my God shall supply all your need according to his riches in glory by Christ Jesus' (Philippians 4:19).

Elisha had been given a double portion of the spirit of Elijah, and, as this chapter unfolds, we see a parallel with 1 Kings 17, the story of Elijah and the widow at Zarephath. Both events took place in the homes of women who had shown hospitality to God's servants. In the first story, God had prepared the heart of a widow to feed Elijah; in the second, a godly man had died, leaving his widow and two orphaned sons in need. Both women were in danger of losing their children: one through starvation, and the other through slavery. Both experienced a miraculous expansion of their provisions through the faithful ministry of the two prophets. It is helpful to see how God used Elisha in meeting this widow's needs.

GOD'S PROVISION (VV. 2–7)

The needs of the widow and of her two sons were met miraculously. Elisha could have made these needs known to the company of the prophets and solicited help from them. God often provides for his servants through the generosity of others. In this case, however, a supernatural provision was made.

THROUGH ELISHA'S FAITH (VV. 2–3)

Like George Müller, Elisha truly believed that God would not let his servant down. His method was not of his own devising. Elisha walked with God, and we can be sure that what he was asking was directly in line with God's will. It may well have seemed almost bizarre to the woman's neighbours when she came asking for empty jars—surely she should have been asking for *full* ones! But Elisha knew what he was doing: he was sharing his faith with her, not his possessions.

THROUGH THE WOMAN'S OBEDIENCE (V. 5)

Like the widow at Zarephath, this woman was required to invest the little she had in order to experience God's miraculous provision. Here is a great principle that operates within the kingdom of God. Even the little we have belongs to him, and he requires us to offer even this so that he can make his provision for us. A boy's lunch, given into the hands of Jesus, fed five thousand men (John 6:1–15). When Jesus saw a widow putting all the money she possessed into the temple offering, he said, 'Assuredly, I say to you that this poor widow has put in more than all those who have given to the treasury' (Mark 12:43). In a parable about stewardship, he said, 'He who is faithful in what is least is faithful also in much' (Luke 16:10). In our deepest need, we may feel that we have very little to offer to God, but our obedience to him is like the little boy's lunch or the widow's two coins.

THROUGH THE USE OF OIL (VV. 5–6)

The miraculous outpouring of the oil into the jars amply provided for the widow so that she could pay her creditors and have enough left to provide for herself and her children. If we look at the way in which oil is used in the Bible, we can see illustrations of that way in which God has provided, and continues to provide, for *all* our needs—especially our salvation—through his Son, Jesus Christ. In the Bible, oil was used in a number of ways:

Firstly, olive oil was commonly used for lighting. When offerings were made in the tabernacle, the priests were instructed to use 'oil for the light, and spices for the anointing oil and for the sweet incense' (Exodus 25:6). In the story of the wise and foolish virgins, 'Those who were foolish took their lamps and took no oil with them, but the wise took oil in their vessels with their lamps' (Matthew 25:3–4). Through Jesus

Christ, God provides light for our pathway (John 1:4; 8:12).

Secondly, oil was an essential ingredient in the diet of the Israelites—especially in the making of bread. Cakes were made of flour mixed with oil. The widow at Zarephath, who ministered to Elijah, was gathering sticks to make such cakes when God's servant found her (1 Kings 17:12). Christ is the Bread of Life for all who believe in him (John 6:50–51).

Thirdly, along with wine, oil was used as a healing agent for wounds (Luke 10:34). It was also to accompany the prayer of faith when praying for the sick (James 5:14–15). Jesus sent his disciples to anoint the sick (Mark 6:13). The presence of oil symbolized gladness (Isaiah 61:3), but its absence indicated sorrow or humiliation (Joel 1:10).

Fourthly, oil was integral to the religious life of Israel. It symbolized the outpouring of God's Spirit upon a person, who was set apart for God's holy purpose. The true prophet of God was one who had received God's anointing for his task. His role was to 'speak forth' the word of God to the people. He was, in effect, the mouthpiece of God to Israel. When Jesus, the Anointed One, entered the synagogue, he chose to establish his authority by reading from the prophet Isaiah:

> The Spirit of the LORD is upon me, because he has anointed me to preach the gospel to the poor; he has sent me to heal the brokenhearted, to proclaim liberty to the captives and recovery of sight to the blind, to set at liberty those who are oppressed; to proclaim the acceptable year of the LORD (Luke 4:18–19; see Isaiah 61).

The priest was the mediator between God and man. He was chosen to offer the sacrifices prescribed by God for cleansing and worship. He was anointed for this task with a sweet-smelling oil made to God's formula especially for this particular task (Exodus 30:22–33).

Kings, too, would receive an anointing at their coronation. When God chose David to succeed Saul as king of Israel, Samuel the prophet was instructed to anoint him. We are told that 'the Spirit of the LORD came upon David from that day forward' (1 Samuel 16:13).

Jesus is the Christ, the Anointed One; the Prophet, who reveals God to man (Deuteronomy 18:18; Luke 7:16; John 6:14); the Priest and Mediator, who offered himself as the sacrifice for our sin (Hebrews 3:1; 4:14; Romans 3:24–25; 1 John 2:2); and the King, who reigns over us and is the ruler of our lives (Ephesians 1:22; 1 Corinthians 15:25).

Jesus! my Shepherd, Brother, Friend
My Prophet, Priest and King,
My Lord, my Life, my Way, my End,
Accept the praise I bring (John Newton).

THE PROVISION WAS GREATER THAN THE NEED (VV. 5–7)

The widow's request was that her debt be paid to prevent her two sons being taken as slaves. With the continual flow of the oil, there was an abundance that provided for her future and that of her sons. The Christian has a similar experience of God's provision in his or her life.

THE SHUNAMMITE (VV. 8–37)

Elisha moved from the home of a poor woman to that of a rich one, but encountered great need there, too.

SHE SHOWED GREAT KINDNESS (VV. 9–10)

Her kindness to the man of God was an expression of her faith and godliness. Kindness is a product of love: 'Love suffers long and is kind' (1 Corinthians 13:4). It is also listed as part of the fruit of the Spirit (Galatians 5:22).

The Shunammite's kindness was expressed through hospitality. She had even set aside a room in her house for the prophet's use whenever he should call. Here is the practical expression of our love for one another in Christ. God calls us to share with his people and to practise hospitality (Romans 12:13). Writing of the last days, Peter instructs the church to 'Be hospitable to one another without grumbling' (1 Peter 4:9). How often have visitors to churches been discouraged because no one was hospitable towards them? On the other hand, many have been brought to a knowledge of Jesus Christ because some have taken the trouble to invite them to their homes.

SHE RECEIVED GREAT BLESSING (VV. 11–17)

Her kindness to God's servant was rewarded. Her need was different from that of the widow (vv. 1–7). Like Sarah (Genesis 16:1–2) and Hannah (1 Samuel 1:5–6) before her, she did not have a child. At first she did not believe Elisha when he prophesied her pregnancy, but she was soon overjoyed at the birth of her son. Like her illustrious predecessors, she too had experienced God's miraculous provision (Genesis 21:1–7; 1 Samuel 1:20).

SHE ENDURED GREAT TRIAL (VV. 18–21)

To lose a child is a great tragedy; to lose one who is a miracle gift from God is beyond human comprehension. We can barely imagine what was going on in the woman's mind as she cradled her dying son in her arms.

There are no pat answers to such things—no easy words that trip off the tongue in explanation. Here is God exercising his sovereignty in a way that is beyond our understanding. Like Job, we can only say, 'The LORD gave, and the LORD has taken away; blessed be the name of the LORD' (Job 1:21). There is no doubt that her son's death broke her heart (v. 27)—she must have felt as if the man of God had played some kind of sick joke on her (v. 28).

SHE SHOWED GREAT FAITH (VV. 22–30)

It is interesting to study her behaviour at this point. She appeared to go into a state of denial of the event that had just taken place, which is not uncommon in the early stages of bereavement. Her words in verses 23 and 26 would seem to support such an interpretation, but for the crucial factor in her behaviour: her faith. In taking the boy's body to the prophet's room, it was as if she was giving him back to God! Her refusal to tell her husband of their son's death was designed to spare him distress, for she believed that the prophet of God would raise the boy from the dead. This was a matter of urgency (v. 24), and any delay in meeting with Elisha would be critical.

SHE EXPERIENCED GREAT JOY (VV. 31–37)

We can only imagine the joy experienced by someone whose child has been brought back from the dead. This woman's faith in God's power, exercised through Elisha, was rewarded. Here was Elisha again operating in the spirit of Elijah (1 Kings

17:17–24). Such demonstrations of God's power over death were exceptional. They pointed to Christ, who is 'the resurrection and the life' (John 11:25). Even he, in his ministry on earth, only raised three people from the dead (Mark 5:21–43; Luke 7:11–17; John 11:38–44). All these were pointing to a greater resurrection that God has promised for all who have a living relationship with him through Jesus Christ (1 Corinthians 15:51–58; 1 Thessalonians 4:13–18).

ELISHA

HE RECEIVED HOSPITALITY GLADLY

It is said that 'It is better to give than to receive'. It is also often easier! If someone offers hospitality, there should also be someone ready and willing to receive it. Jesus instructed his disciples to do just that (Luke 10:5–9). The life of Elisha demonstrates a willingness to do this. It is easy to stifle a person's gift by refusing to accept the benefits from it. Fellowship is a partnership in an enterprise. Partners give and take, both benefiting from the joint undertaking.

HE LONGED TO BLESS

Throughout this story we see a man of God who is actively seeking to bring God's blessing to another. Elisha instructed Gehazi to find out whether the Shunammite had any need that he could meet (vv. 11–13). When the woman later came to him at Carmel he sent his servant to see that all was well before hearing of the death of her son (vv. 25–26). God's prophet did not just sit back and wait for a need to arise, he actively looked for those whom he could bless. Surely this is a lesson to the church.

HE WALKED WITH GOD

Throughout this story Elisha was sure of what he needed to do. He was clear in his instructions to Gehazi and never showed a flicker of doubt as he gave himself fully to the task of restoring the boy to his parents. He knew that there was a time to involve others and a time to be alone with God. How did he attain such wisdom? Surely it was because he walked with God and listened carefully to God's instructions. Here was a man who was always willing to do things God's way!

Here were two women who, in their different ways and in accordance with their gifts, gave themselves wholeheartedly to God's service. And with them was a man of God who, equally wholeheartedly, entered into their lives to bring God's blessing and power.

For further study ▶

FOR FURTHER STUDY

1. *Think about the prominence the Bible gives to the gift of hospitality (see Romans 12:9–13; 1 Timothy 3:2; 5:9–10; Titus 1:7–9; 1 Peter 4:9–10).*

2. *Draw out the parallels between the provision made for the Shunammite and that made for the widow at Zarephath (1 Kings 17).*

FOR FURTHER STUDY

1. *Gethsemene was a place where olives were gathered and pressed. How do the ministry and death of Jesus relate to the uses of oil mentioned in this chapter? (See Matthew 26:36–56; Mark 14:32–50.)*

2. *What can we learn from the trials of the widow of Zarephath and the Shunammite?*

3. *What benefits do trials have for the Christian? (See James 1:3–4.)*

6 Purification and multiplication

2 Kings 4:38–44

This passage teaches that God is able to purify that which has become polluted and life threatening—and multiply that which is good and life giving. Sin pollutes every part of our being. Some things seem good and acceptable to us, but God knows the harm that these things will do to our lives. Through confession and faith in the finished work of Christ we find cleansing. Where there is a need, God is able to do 'exceedingly abundantly above all that we ask or think' (Ephesians 3:20).

PURIFICATION (VV. 38–41)

As I walk through the woods near my home I am always delighted to stumble upon some wild fungi. I often dream of gathering them in a basket, taking them home and cooking them. I have even bought a book to enable me to identify the edible, the inedible and the poisonous. The trouble is, when I take my book into the woods, the fungi on the ground never accurately resemble the pictures on the pages, so they remain unharvested. I return home with an unfulfilled dream!

The prophet Elisha had returned to Gilgal and, to quote Alfred Edersheim,

Times and scenes have sadly changed. Once more has a terrible drought withered the land, and famine and misery have swept over the people. Elisha is no longer at Mount Carmel, nor the Shunammite in her great, hospitable house. The famine has driven her from Shunem; and the famine has determined Elisha once more to seek out the sons of the prophets at Gilgal. In their company our narrative finds him, this time engaged in his favourite occupation of instructing them in the word and in the ways of God.[1]

PAVED WITH GOOD INTENTIONS

A proverb, dating back to the sixteenth century, tells us that 'The road to hell is paved with good intentions'. Before we can *do* what is right we must *know* what is right. The disciple of Elisha who went out into the field to gather wild herbs certainly had good intentions. The wild gourds looked appetizing, and even if none of the company of prophets knew what they were, it would be assumed that the cook knew his onions! One sip of the soup, however, was enough to dispel their confidence in him. There was 'death in the pot'.

There are some who would say, 'It doesn't really matter what you believe as long as you are sincere.' Some might go further and conclude that, because God looks on the heart, our intentions are more important than our actions. There is, of course, an element of truth in this, but it is just a part of the whole truth. Actions really matter. If we intend to do what is right, it is essential that we know what is right! The prophet who gathered the wild vegetables to feed his fellows must have been delighted when he returned to the camp with his crop—but in this case a knowledge of botany would have been handy, too!

The Bible is full of instruction as to the effect of sin upon our lives and the lives of others. God has gone to great lengths to inform us of and illustrate the fatal consequences of disobedience to his law. 'There is a way that seems right to a man, but its end is the way of death' (Proverbs 14:12).

THE EXTRAORDINARY IN THE ORDINARY

God's people are not exempt from the effects of the sin of the world. With few exceptions (Mark 16:9–20; Acts 28:1–6) we are subject to the diseases common to all men and ultimately to death. We are, however, citizens of the kingdom of God, and, in his sovereignty, God can overrule for his own purpose and glory. He sometimes chooses to demonstrate this by using what is ordinary in an extraordinary way.

When the Israelites were gasping for water in the Wilderness of Shur and came to Marah, the water was undrinkable. God commanded Moses to cast a piece of wood into the water to make it sweet to the taste (Exodus 15:22–27). Earlier in Elisha's ministry he had thrown a bowl of salt into the well at Jericho and restored the city's water supply (2 Kings 2:19–21).

God's people are not exempt from trials and tribulations. Yet such things are surely permitted by God and used by him for his eternal purpose. Often such trials are essential for our sanctification. We often learn much more about ourselves and our relationship with God during these times than we do in times of great blessing.

The prophets were hungry, but the stew was polluted. In the ordinary way, a handful of flour would only thicken the mess, but here the flour turned what was poisonous into a life-giving provision. Again, Elisha demonstrated God's mighty power to his people.

POISONED BY SIN

There is 'death in the pot' for a mankind that is poisoned by sin. 'The soul who sins shall die' (Ezekiel 18:20). 'The wages of sin is death' (Romans 6:23). The casting of flour into the pot can be seen as a picture of Christ, the antidote to sin and death! In Christ, God provided the 'flour' to be cast into the poisoned pot of a sinful world. Through his perfect life and atoning death he became the Bread of Life for those who would be reconciled to God through him (John 6:32–35).

Such is the power of God that even the presence of a godly person can have a saving effect on those around. If ten righteous men had been found in the sinful city of Sodom, God would have spared it from destruction (Genesis 18:32). Even within a marriage a believing spouse and parent brings blessing upon the whole family (1 Corinthians 7:12–14).

MULTIPLICATION (VV. 42–44)

I once heard a retired missionary recount an experience during his long ministry in South East Asia. He had been labouring in a remote village in an area where a number of colleagues were in a similar situation. Cut off from outside sources, he had no choice but to eat the local food—rice, rice and even more rice, supplemented sometimes by whatever could be found growing around his primitive lodgings. News reached him that another missionary had obtained a packet of biscuits (cookies) and was willing to share them with his friends. After a long and arduous trek through hostile jungle he reached the appointed place to discover that he was the last one of the party to arrive. As they passed the packet round, each one giving thanks to God, the effect was, as he later described it, 'almost sacramental'—a visible sign of an invisible grace. The journey home brought joy to his heart—and to his stomach!

A WELCOME CHANGE OF DIET

The purified stew was life-giving sustenance for the company of the prophets. But now the visit from a man from Baal Shalisha brought a welcome change to their diet. He had with him twenty loaves of barley bread and some new grain. The company, however, were confronted with a new problem. The food was good, but the quantity was not sufficient. Once more, God's servant Elisha was able to intervene and demonstrate the all-sufficient power of God. What took place was similar to other events recorded in the Bible:

Elisha's mentor, Elijah, had been faced with a similar problem. At Zarephath, a widow had only sufficient oil and flour to bake one last meal for herself and her son. Through Elijah, God promised the woman continual multiplication of the oil and flour until the famine was over, and that she could then rely on natural resources to feed herself and her son (1 Kings 17:7–16).

What the Old Testament prophets were able to do, Jesus did in abundance. On two occasions, faced with thousands of hungry people, he was able to multiply a few loaves and fish to more than satisfy their hunger (Matthew 15:29–39; Mark 8:1–13; Matthew 14:13–21; Mark 6:30–44; Luke 9:10–17).

SUFFICIENT GRACE

Throughout history, God has demonstrated the sufficiency of his grace, often testing the faith of his people. The diaries of George Müller record the way in which God wonderfully provided for the needs of the orphans in his care. Müller's faith was tested as provision for each day would often arrive just in the nick of time. Each new day would reveal another need and drive the saintly pastor from Bristol to his knees in faithful petition.

The Israelites in the wilderness experienced the same daily provision as they were supplied with manna from heaven. God revealed that this was to humble and test them: 'So he humbled you, allowed you to hunger, and fed you with manna which you did not know nor did your fathers know, that he might make you know that man shall not live by bread alone; but man lives by every word that proceeds from the mouth of the LORD' (Deuteronomy 8:3).

It is easy for us to see this and rejoice in it when God provides the immediate needs that we have encountered and illustrated in this chapter so far. But sometimes his provision goes beyond our understanding and meets a deeper need that only he can see. The apostle Paul experienced this when he was troubled by what he described as a 'thorn in the flesh'. We do not know what this thorn was, but Paul, being a man of faith, pleaded with God three times to take it away. God's answer was simply, 'My grace is sufficient for you, for my strength is made perfect in weakness.' Was Paul disappointed? Did he feel that God had let him down? Far from it! His response was, 'Therefore most gladly I will rather boast in my infirmities, that the power of Christ may rest upon me' (2 Corinthians 12:7–9).

ABUNDANT PROVISION

In all the instances that we have recorded in this chapter, God's provision has exceeded the need. When Jesus referred to the way in which his Father cared for the whole of creation, he spoke of a greater care for his people (Luke 12:22–28). In the doxology that divides the two sections of Paul's letter to the Ephesians, the apostle wrote of 'him who is able to do exceedingly abundantly above all that we ask or think' (Ephesians 3:20).

I started attending a church as a young man seeking peace for a troubled soul. The pastor faithfully preached the gospel, and I soon came under conviction of sin and realized my need to repent and trust Christ as my Saviour. During this period I was also fascinated by the pastor's pulpit prayers that often contained those words of Paul. However, I gave no indication as to what was happening inside me—even though I knew that the pastor was praying for my conversion. He left the church for other Christian work and died shortly afterwards, his prayers still unanswered. Five years later I was converted, and five years after that I was occupying his pulpit!

For further study ▶

FOR FURTHER STUDY

1. *Give some spiritual instances of multiplication (e.g. Ephesians 3:20; Acts 2:47; 4:4, etc.).*

2. *Read the following Bible passages: Romans 3:24; 5:20; 6:14; 11:6; 2 Corinthians 12:9; Ephesians 2:5; 2 Thessalonians 2:16. What do they tell us about grace?*

FOR FURTHER STUDY

1. *Is sincerity a sufficient sign of salvation? If not, what is?*

2. *How does sin 'poison' a person, and how can its effects be seen in a person's life?*

Notes

1. Ibid. p. 115.

7 I did it my way

2 Kings 5:1–27

One of the most popular pieces of music played at cremations these days is the song *My Way*. As the coffin is removed from sight, the mourners make their sad way out of the chapel to the sound of Frank Sinatra's voice fading in the distance singing, 'I did it my way'. It has become a humanist hymn—a kind of final declaration of man's independence.

This passage is the story of a man who learned that 'doing it my way' does not work. But when he humbled himself before God and did it God's way, he unleashed the awesome power of God into his life.

Many centuries later, the apostle Peter wrote, 'Therefore humble yourselves under the mighty hand of God, that he may exalt you in due time' (1 Peter 5:6).

I DID IT MY WAY

NAAMAN (VV. 1–3)

Naaman was the kind of man people look up to; the sort of man you would want to be leading the army during a time of war. His bravery and determination were without question, and they were tempered by an integrity that brought respect and affection from king and servant girl alike. His presence at the head of the ranks of the Syrian army even brought God's blessing!

But he was also a man in great need. He was a leper! It is at times like this that a man or woman realizes that life is fragile, and that any kind of help must be sought; but for Naaman the only way he knew was the way of the world. At such a time it was helpful to have friends in high places. News reached him that there was a prophet in Israel who had the power to heal. The world abounds with 'healers', and although any port in a storm might bring his troubled mind and diseased body into calmer waters, this particular 'port' was Israel, Syria's enemy! Maybe the king would help him.

THE KING OF SYRIA (VV. 4–6)

During this period, Syria (a Greek name for Aram) and Israel were engaged in some fierce and bloody conflicts. For a period of about 130 years the Syrians were ruled by the Ben-Hadad dynasty. During the reign of Asa, king of Judah, the Syrians were bribed to abandon their treaty with Israel, side with the Judeans and attack a number of Israelite cities (1 Kings 15:18–20). During the time of Elijah, they were defeated by the armies of King Ahab (1 Kings 20). Later, Ahab perished in battle against the Syrians, when an arrow pierced him between the joints of his armour (1 Kings 22:29–40).

Naaman was soon on his way to Israel bearing a letter of introduction to the king of Israel. The Syrian king was used to giving and receiving bribes. It was the way things were done—allegiances made and favours granted between the courts of the ancient world. Naaman's well-being was crucial to the king's success in battle, so it would have taken a freight train to shift the silver and gold that was intended to sway the heart and mind of Israel's king. Faith healing can be a lucrative business.

THE KING OF ISRAEL (V. 7)

The greedy heart of the king of Israel would have welcomed the money, but his worldly-wise mind had spotted a trap. The terms on which the money had been given were impossible. Ancient kings were said to have the healing touch, but surely the king of Syria did not believe that he could do anything for his commander-in-chief? In blind panic, he tore his clothes. As Shakespeare once wrote, 'Uneasy lies the head that wears a crown.'[1] The bearer of the letter was the man who was thought to have fired the fatal arrow that killed the king of Israel's father; was he now on an errand to destroy the whole family? Bribes were common in those days; so was regicide!

While the king and his counsellors feverishly looked for a way out of this dangerous dilemma, the God who had been in control from the very beginning was about to show his hand.

I DID IT GOD'S WAY

While the king looked for the reason behind the unwelcome visit of the Syrian general, he was blind to the real reason for Naaman's presence in his court. It was born, not in the mind of a devious Syrian king, but in the simple faith of an Israelite servant girl.

THE FAITHFUL WITNESSES (VV. 2–3,8)

A missionary on a remote island once tried in vain to obtain an audience with the island's ruler. Time after time, her attempts were rebuffed. One day, she was attacked in the street and her bag was stolen. It contained her papers, her money and her Bible. She reported it to the local authorities, but they showed little interest. Some time later, she was summoned to the ruler's home. On arrival, she was treated with great courtesy and shown into the ruler's presence. After the usual pleasantries, he reached out and returned her bag. The thieves had thrown it over the wall of his compound. The money and the Bible were missing, but her papers were intact. She noticed that the Bible was on a small table next to the ruler. He had been reading it, and had sent for her to question her about some of the passages that intrigued him. She was able to share with him the way of salvation. So often, things that at first appearance spell disaster are, in the end, God's means of giving opportunity to witness.

So it was in the case of the Israelite girl. She had been taken from her home and family by a Syrian raiding party—a spoil of war. Instead of the rape and abuse that was generally meted out to young female prisoners, Naaman and his wife had treated her kindly. She now wanted to show her gratitude by telling Naaman about God's prophet in Israel. God's ways are past finding out (Romans 11:33). The disaster that had befallen her young life was the means by which God was to demonstrate his mighty power—and cement her place in history.

The girl was confident that Elisha would be able to heal Naaman's leprosy. Elisha's message to the king ('Please let him come to me, and he shall know that there is a prophet in Israel', v. 8) demonstrated the same confidence. The girl was not putting her trust in man; neither was the prophet exhibiting a swaggering self-assurance. Both knew that it was God alone, working through his servant, who could heal the Syrian commander.

Here we have a good example of how we are to view the work of God in the life of the church and the community around us. We too must recognize those whom God has called and equipped to further the work of his kingdom. They bear an awesome responsibility. We must also, like Elisha, recognize and accept with all humility what God has called and equipped us to do. Faith demonstrates a holy boldness by taking personal responsibility for the work of God in us!

THE OBEDIENCE OF NAAMAN (V. 14)

God doesn't allow us to be the scriptwriter for his scenarios. Naaman thought he knew exactly how the prophet was going to heal him (vv. 11–12). Due recognition of his status would be given, and an elaborate but dignified gesture would be made on his behalf. Disappointment and anger are often the first things we encounter when God is about to do a great work in us. The humbling process can be painful and we often need the wise counsel of others to put us back on track (v. 13). Naaman listened, obeyed the prophet's command, and the leprosy was gone!

God's way is the only way. Pride can keep a person enslaved in the leprosy of sin and unbelief. God's way is the only prescription that will bring a cure. The cross is foolishness to man, but it is God's power for salvation. Repentance and faith in God's Son go against man's religious instinct to work out that salvation for himself, but God demands this from all who would enter his kingdom. Baptism drowns our dignity, but it is

God's way of witness to our oneness in him and with our fellow believers.

The consequences of Naaman's healing are noted in this chapter to great effect upon the reader. Here we see the gratitude of one man; the godliness of another; and the greed of one who seeks to exploit, for his own purpose, the great work that God has done.

GRATITUDE (VV. 15–19)

There was a profound change in Naaman. Five times in these verses he refers to himself as Elisha's servant. When we compare this with his previous arrogance we can see that God had dealt with more than just his leprosy. There is a kind of beautiful naivety about the way in which he expressed the change. He came from a different culture and had yet to learn the ways of God's people.

He openly declared his faith in God, and wanted to express his gratitude in the only way he knew how: by giving a gift to Elisha. The prophet's refusal may have hurt him, but he was to learn the right way to do these things. A new convert may often make a gesture that is completely inappropriate, but God sees the intention, and God's people must seek to do the same.

The living relationship that Naaman now had with God brought a desire to worship him. But his Syrian background limited any understanding he had about true worship. Gods were territorial. They had their places of inhabitance. It was natural that the Syrian commander should want to take back some of the earth from the place where they were standing, so that he could continue to worship the one true God when he got back home. Like the woman from Samaria, he had to learn that 'God is Spirit, and those who worship him must worship in spirit and truth' (John 4:24).

Naaman also had a desire to honour God on his return to his post as commander of the Syrian army (v. 18). There is a temptation to feel disappointed by this verse. Naaman seemed to lack total commitment—he appeared to want a compromise. We need, however, to read more carefully before we jump to conclusions. He *was* committed to the one true God, but he was going to face a major problem when he got back to work, and he needed the prophet's counsel. Dale Ralph Davis sums this up superbly:

> Superficially Naaman's request might give ground to some to rag on Naaman's incomplete commitment. One might hold forth here on 'the peril of small compromise' or harangue folks about the disappointment of 90 percent commitment. But the fact is that Elisha sent Naaman off in peace (v. 19a) and didn't seem overly concerned about the matter, perhaps because Naaman was miles ahead of scores of Israelites. Note, positively, what verse 18 shows. It shows a sensitive conscience. Here is a man who feels the rub between his exclusive allegiance to Yahweh and the expectations of his work place. And it bothers him. Would that Bethel-visiting or Baal-kissing Israelites were bothered like this! Would that they could have the uneasy conscience of this gentile! Would that apparent inconsistencies drove them to seek pardon![2]

GODLINESS (VV. 16,19,26–27)

As far as Elisha was concerned, Naaman's transformation was solely for God's glory (v. 16). To accept a gift in this situation would draw attention to the vessel and not to the source of the miracle. He had been prepared to take a prominent place as the means through which God would do his great work, but now that it was done there was only room on the stage for one person: the God of Israel.

Elisha's blessing on Naaman indicated his wisdom in dealing with the man's concern about the problems that he would face back in Syria. He detected Naaman's sincerity and trusted that God would be honoured when the Syrian commander resumed his duties.

The instrument of Naaman's blessing was also prepared to be the instrument of his servant Gehazi's judgement. This was not because his servant had let *him* down, but because Gehazi's action was an affront to the honour of his righteous God.

Those who are godly seek only God's glory. Their delight is in the Lord and they are not concerned with the blessings, both actual and potential, that might fall upon them as a result of their service. They are sensitive to the way in which the Lord is dealing with others. They seek to understand the particular difficulties of others, and to encourage and bless them, confident that the one who has begun a good work in them will perform it. At the same time, godly people do not shrink from the responsibility of declaring God's righteous judgement upon sinners.

GREED (VV. 19–27)

'Dead flies putrefy the perfumer's ointment, and cause it to give off a foul odour (Ecclesiastes 10:1). As Naaman made his way back to Syria and the perfume of his praise and Elisha's godliness ascended into heaven, a dead fly dropped into the ointment in the person of Gehazi. Like Judas, he could not rise beyond the petty mindedness of his fallen thinking (John 12:1–8). After all, Naaman was rich, he was grateful and he had already offered a gift; why not give him the opportunity to show his gratitude in a tangible way? Gehazi's actions brought dishonour upon Elisha and the judgement of the God whom he had disobeyed upon Gehazi.

The trouble with Gehazi was that his fallen reasoning brought him into direct conflict with God's commandment. The Bible tells us that 'There is a way that seems right to a man, but its end is the way of death' (Proverbs 16:25). Gehazi could do things his way or God's way; he chose his way. The actions that followed revealed that he was motivated by his own greed and not by God's glory. He deceived Naaman and lied to Elisha.

Sin gets us like that. At the outset, our actions may seem reasonable and justifiable. But if they are in conflict with the revealed will of God they can only be perpetuated by further sin. One lie will have to be supported by a whole string of them!

Gehazi's foolishness was amplified by his knowledge of the one to whom he was lying. He had witnessed the way in which God had already revealed things to the prophet. Such is the power of sin that a man can even believe that he can lie to God.

The outcome was inevitable. Elisha saw through Gehazi's wicked plan and pronounced God's judgement on him. The leprosy washed away in the river Jordan would now cling to him and his descendants. God is holy, and judges a man in righteousness. Sin is pernicious and, even when forgiven, can have devastating consequences.

FOR FURTHER STUDY

***1.** Read Leviticus 13–14; 2 Kings 5; Matthew 10:8; Mark 1:40; and Luke 5:12–13. What parallels can be drawn between leprosy and sin?*
***2.** Recall other instances in the Bible when God's people have been put into desperate situations in order to witness to his grace.*

FOR FURTHER STUDY

***1.** Has pride kept you from experiencing a work of God in your life? What would you need to do to emulate Naaman's obedience?*
***2.** What lessons can the Christian worker learn from Elisha's behaviour?*

Notes

1. **William Shakespeare,** *Henry IV, Part 2*.
2. **Dale Ralph Davis,** *2 Kings: The Power and the Fury*, (Fearn, Tain: Christian Focus Publications, 2005), p. 93.

8 Of mice and men

2 Kings 6:1–23

The Scottish poet Robert Burns' famous lines, 'The best laid schemes o' mice an' men/ Gang aft agley' ('The best-laid plans of mice and men go oft awry'), were apparently an apology to a mouse after having ploughed up its nest; they sum up the frustration and futility of thinking that things will always go according to plan. This chapter reveals how God's provision will often frustrate our understanding of how he is going to work things out. All things will work together for good, but not necessarily in the order in which we place them.

GOD'S PROVISION FOR HIS PEOPLE (VV. 1–7)

AN APPROACHABLE LEADER (VV. 1–4)

Most Christian leaders would be delighted with the problem now facing Elisha. His work among the prophets had outgrown the premises. Not averse to hard work—like Robert Burns, Elisha was a ploughman—he accompanied his students to oversee and assist in the building of new quarters. The active verbs of the passage epitomize the leadership of Christ over his church: '*Go*'; 'I will *go*'; 'So he *went* with them.' Christ commands his people to *go* into the world with the gospel (Matthew 28:19); he promises his presence (Matthew 28:20);

and the ongoing experience of his people is, 'Christ in you, the hope of glory' (Colossians 1:27).

Elisha was an approachable 'hands-on' leader. Christ, as head of his church, is like his people in every way except for sin. He is approachable in all situations, 'that we may obtain mercy and find grace to help in time of need' (Hebrews 4:14–16). As the story unfolds in 2 Kings 6:1–7, it becomes clear that such help was needed by one of the prophets!

PANIC AND POWER (VV. 5–7)

Life is full of embarrassments. You sell a car to a friend and it breaks down on the journey home. It always seems to be the borrowed lawnmower that hits the one unseen stone on your lawn. Such was the fate of one of the prophets. The axe he was using fell apart as he enthusiastically swung it, and the axe head plunged deep into the river. Where else would a borrowed axe head fall? But Elisha was there as the instrument of God's provision. The miracle was a demonstration not just of God's almighty power, but also of his infinite providential care.

Have you noticed the detailed way in which God provides for his people? Not even a sparrow falls to the ground unnoticed (Matthew 10:29). When Jesus instructs us not to worry, he draws our attention to the way in which even flowers and birds are under divine care (Matthew 6:25–34). Christ's post-resurrection ministry to his disciples even included a cooked breakfast (John 21:1–14)!

GOD'S PROTECTION OF HIS PEOPLE (VV. 8–23)

The scene now shifts from one man's embarrassment to a plot

to overthrow the king of Israel and enslave the whole people of God. 'He who is in you is greater than he who is in the world' (1 John 4:4). Alfred Edersheim says,

> From every seeming evil, as from a root deep buried in the ground, springs high and lasting good; and if 'the whole creation groaneth and travaileth in pain together', it is in the birth-throes of a holier and better life than earth has yet witnessed. God is not merely in heaven: he reigneth; and there is not a secret design whispered in the council-chamber of Ben-Hadad which is not known to him, or which can come at unawares upon his cause or people.[1]

As the saying goes: 'Man proposes, God disposes.'

SATAN'S PLAN (VV. 8,13–14)

Satan intends to bring hurt upon the work of the kingdom of God. But ultimately the cause of God will always triumph. It is the godly who bear the brunt of his attack. Satan believed that, if he could remove the blessings that God had abundantly bestowed upon Job, then Job would ultimately curse God (Job 1:6–12). He sought to make Judas Iscariot a pawn in his game plan to bring about the fall of the King of kings (Luke 22:3–6). The church must be vigilant, 'lest Satan should take advantage of us; for we are not ignorant of his devices' (2 Corinthians 2:11).

GOD'S KNOWLEDGE (VV. 9–12)

Nothing occurs outside the knowledge of the omniscient God. Everything in the conversation that took place in the court of the king of Syria was relayed to the king of Israel—even the words uttered in his own bedroom! No bugging device was available nor necessary. It can be frightening for a Christian to realize that he or she is a target for Satan's attack, but we can be confident in the knowledge that God knows more than Satan can ever know and has already made provision for the outcome—even if such an attack may in the short term seem to be successful.

The apostle Peter was emphatic in his assertion that he was prepared to go to prison, even to death, for the sake of his Lord. Jesus told him that, on the contrary, he was going to deny him. Before doing this, however, Jesus revealed something known by God but unknown to Peter: 'Simon, Simon! Indeed, Satan has asked for you, that he may sift you as wheat. But I have prayed for you, that your faith should not fail; and when you have returned to me, strengthen your brethren' (Luke 22:31–32). Jesus was not just aware of what was going to take place, but he had also already made provision for Peter's restoration.

GOD'S POWER (VV. 15–20)

We are often overwhelmed by the appearance of forces massed against us. Everything within society seems to be in the control of the godless, militating against our desire to walk with God. We often feel defeated by the trials and tribulations of this life and can sympathize with the cry of Elisha's servant: 'Alas, my master! What shall we do?' (v. 15).

At such times we need to turn to the Word of God to get his perspective. The Bible opens our eyes to the 'horses and chariots of fire' that surround God's people. A kind of poetic justice now occurs within the narrative. The God who opened the eyes of his servant then incapacitated his enemies with blindness and took them captive (vv. 18–20).

The Christian's victory, and God's provision for that victory, is to be found in the place of the greatest victory—the cross. It was there that Satan suffered his eternal defeat, and it is there that the sinner finds deliverance from death and judgement. Darkness covered the whole earth as Jesus 'who knew no sin [was made] to be sin for us, that we might become the righteousness of God in him' (2 Corinthians 5:21). In his atoning death, Jesus forsook the very protection that God has afforded his people: 'Or do you think that I cannot now pray to my Father, and he will provide me with more than twelve legions of angels? How then could the Scriptures be fulfilled, that it must happen thus?' (Matthew 26:53–54).

GOD'S MERCY (VV. 21–23)

As the Syrian army lay captive before his, the king of Israel must have remembered the disobedience of Ahab, who had made a treaty with Ben-Hadad instead of killing him as God had commanded (1 Kings 20:35–43). His first inclination was to kill them, but he was instructed by Elisha to spare them and treat them kindly. God's will in these matters is paramount. He reveals himself to be a God of holiness and judgement—but also a God of grace and mercy. It is for him to decide the fate of the sinner, not us. 'If it is possible, as much as depends on you, live peaceably with all men. Beloved, do not avenge yourselves, but rather give place to wrath; for it is written, "Vengeance is mine, I will repay," says the Lord' (Romans 12:18–19).

When Satan attacks us through our personal sin, we must be ruthless in dealing with ourselves. But when he attacks us through our relationships with others, we must be wise and gracious in dealing with them. Although the Christian deserves judgement and punishment, when he or she comes to Christ, mercy is given:

> For we ourselves were also once foolish, disobedient, deceived, serving various lusts and pleasures, living in malice and envy, hateful and hating one another. But when the kindness and the love of God our Saviour toward man appeared, not by works of righteousness which we have done, but according to his mercy he saved us, through the washing of regeneration and renewing of the Holy Spirit, whom he poured out on us abundantly through Jesus Christ our Saviour (Titus 3:3–6).

As Christians we are instructed to love our enemies, do good to them and pray for them (Matthew 5:44). Paul entreats us to feed our enemies and give them a drink if they are hungry and thirsty. In doing so, we 'will heap coals of fire on [their] head' (Romans 12:20). These acts of benevolence will shame them and may well bring about a conviction of sin that may abound to their salvation. When Abraham Lincoln became President of the United States in 1861, Edwin M. Stanton treated him with contempt. He referred to Lincoln as a 'low cunning clown', and nicknamed him 'The original gorilla'. The president refused to retaliate. In fact, he appointed Stanton as his War Minister on the strength of his obvious ability to do the job well, and treated him with the utmost respect and courtesy. After many years, the night came when Lincoln was assassinated. In the room where his body lay, Stanton looked down at the dead president and was heard to say through his tears, 'There lies the greatest ruler the world has ever seen.' Lincoln's patience with Stanton had won through in the end.

God's care for his people is both personal and global. He can recover an axe head as well as save a nation from disaster. In the small and in the great, the Christian has the security of God's providential care throughout life and into eternity. As the hymn writer put it:

Enough: this covers all my wants;
And so I rest!
For what I cannot, he can see,
And in his care I saved shall be,
For ever blest, for ever blest (Joseph Parker).

For further study ▶

FOR FURTHER STUDY

1. *Read Matthew 6:25–34; 10:29; John 21:1–14. How is God's provision seen in your current circumstances? Give thanks for all you discover.*

2. *In his letter to the Philippians, Paul rejoices in God's provision for his life and ministry. What does Philippians 4 tell us about the nature of this provision and the way in which it is made?*

FOR FURTHER STUDY

1. *Think about God's knowledge (1 Kings 8:29; Psalm 139:1–16; John 21:17; Hebrews 4:13); power (Genesis 18:14; Jeremiah 32:27; Zechariah 8:6; Matthew 3:9; 26:53); and mercy (Luke 1:54,72,78; Romans 9:16–18; 15:9; Ephesians 2:4–5). How can these verses help in thwarting Satan's attacks on your life?*

2. *Is there anyone like Ben-Hadad or Edwin M. Stanton in your life? How can you deal with him or her in a godly and loving way?*

Notes

1. **Edersheim,** *Practical Truths*, p. 197.

9 Desolation and deliverance

2 Kings 6:24–7:20

The king of Israel had been obedient to God and had spared the Syrian army in spite of his natural inclination to slaughter them. As a result of his benevolence, Israel was no longer troubled by Syrian raiding parties entering their territory. But now the king was facing a greater threat. Ben-Hadad had gathered his troops together, and the capital city of Israel, Samaria, was now under siege. The king may well have been forgiven for believing that he had made a big mistake in doing what Elisha had instructed! But God had already planned an even greater deliverance for his people. First, though, they had to go through one of the greatest of all scourges that face mankind—famine.

History is littered with chilling accounts of famines that have killed millions of people because of drought, crop failure and war. As I write, over 850 million people are hungry and, every day, more than 16,000 children die from hunger-related causes—one child every five seconds. Scenes depicted on our television screens strike horror into our hearts as we see the results of this devastation. Similarly, the account of the siege and famine in Samaria reveals the effects of starvation, but it goes on to show that God had not deserted his people; his word still goes forth and delivers them.

Later, Amos prophesied a greater famine:

'Behold, the days are coming,' says the Lord GOD, 'that I will send a famine on the land, not a famine of bread, nor a thirst for water, but of hearing the words of the LORD. They shall wander from sea to sea, and from north to east; they shall run to and fro, seeking the word of the LORD, but shall not find it' (Amos 8:11–12).

THE NATURE AND POWER OF SUFFERING (6:24–33)

FAMINE—A MILITARY STRATEGY (VV. 24–25)

In June 1941, the German army was heading swiftly and mercilessly towards the Soviet city of Leningrad (now St Petersburg). By September they had surrounded it. What followed was a human tragedy of gigantic proportion. The 2.8 million civilians (including about 400,000 children), plus troops, who inhabited the city endured a long and devastating siege. By the winter of 1941/42 there was no heating, no water supply, almost no electricity and very little food. In January 1942, in the depths of an unusually cold winter, the lowest food rations in the city were only 125 grams (about 4 oz) of bread per day. In just two months, January and February 1942, 200,000 people died of cold and starvation. Still they did not surrender.

In spite of the deprivation and death that surrounded them, the citizens of Leningrad continued to defy the German army. Several thousand even managed to escape across Lake Ladoga. In January 1943, the siege was broken and a year later, on 27 January 1944, it was fully lifted. At least 641,000 people had died in Leningrad during the siege (some estimates put this figure at 800,000). Most of them were buried in mass graves in different cemeteries. The siege had lasted for about 900 days.

THE HOPELESSNESS AND HELPLESSNESS OF FAMINE (VV. 26–30)

The siege of Samaria by the Syrians soon bit. Not only did the people resort to eating donkeys' heads, they were also paying through the nose to do it (v. 25)! 'Dove droppings' may well have been a popular name for some other kind of food, probably carob pods.

During famine, survival and morality can be in intense conflict. When people are faced with a desperate struggle for survival, the tenderest feelings of human nature can become blunt and demoralized. Some, like the women who argued over their cannibalistic agreement (vv. 28–29), even put their own physical survival above their maternal inclinations. Famine also renders the most powerful powerless. Even the king looked down in helplessness and despair upon the two women who cried out to him for justice, one desperate to save her son and the other desperate to eat him (vv. 27,30)!

THE INNOCENT ARE OFTEN BLAMED FOR THE SUFFERING (VV. 31–33)

In such situations people will often look for someone to blame. This does nothing to alleviate the physical suffering but acts as a temporary palliative for the bitterness and anger of the sufferer. The king's anger was directed towards Elisha, and through him to God. It is so easy to make God the ultimate target—after all, isn't he the one who has the ultimate control of events in this world? But in spite of his temporary obedience, the king had ruled over a rebellious people who were now facing God's judgement—a judgement that would lead to their deliverance.

GOD'S WARNING TO ISRAEL

God had been patient with Israel, but what had been prophesied long before was now being fulfilled:

And after all this, if you do not obey me, but walk contrary to me, then I also will walk contrary to you in fury; and I, even I, will chastise you seven times for your sins. You shall eat the flesh of your sons, and you shall eat the flesh of your daughters (Leviticus 26:27–29).

They shall besiege you at all your gates until your high and fortified walls, in which you trust, come down throughout all your land; and they shall besiege you at all your gates throughout all your land which the LORD your God has given you. You shall eat the fruit of your own body, the flesh of your sons and your daughters whom the LORD your God has given you, in the siege and desperate straits in which your enemy shall distress you. The sensitive and very refined man among you will be hostile toward his brother, toward the wife of his bosom, and toward the rest of his children whom he leaves behind, so that he will not give any of them the flesh of his children whom he will eat, because he has nothing left in the siege and desperate straits in which your enemy shall distress you at all your gates. The tender and delicate woman among you, who would not venture to set the sole of her foot on the ground because of her delicateness and sensitivity, will refuse to the husband of her bosom, and to her son and her daughter, her placenta which comes out from between her feet and her children whom she bears; for she will eat them secretly for lack of everything in the siege and desperate straits in which your enemy shall distress you at all your gates (Deuteronomy 28:52–57).

GOD'S DELIVERANCE FROM SUFFERING (7:1–20)

The God who brings judgement also promises blessing. The judgement upon a disobedient nation had been prophesied and was now being fulfilled, but this was not the last word from God. He who is rich in mercy, and who had allowed this calamity to come upon his people, would now provide for their deliverance. The impatient king was now addressed by a man who knew that God's time had come and who, like his predecessor Elijah, knew no fear in proclaiming the word of God. 'So shall my word be that goes forth from my mouth; it shall not return to me void, but it shall accomplish what I please, and it shall prosper in the thing for which I sent it' (Isaiah 55:11).

THE CONFIDENCE OF ELISHA IN PROCLAIMING GOD'S MESSAGE (V. 1)

God's message to Israel was emphatic and accurately predictive. Elisha was the true prophet of God and spoke God's word into the situation. There was no place for vague promises of deliverance, or even encouragement to trust that God had not abandoned his people. Elisha told them exactly what would happen, when it would happen and where it would happen: 'Tomorrow about this time a seah of fine flour shall be sold for a shekel, and two seahs of barley for a shekel, at the gate of Samaria.' The 'whats', 'wheres' and 'whens' are the marks of God's prophecy throughout the Bible, particularly glorious in the promise of his greatest provision: a Saviour!

Thus, the preacher and teacher can proclaim God's word boldly, and the Bible reader can trust that every prophecy of Scripture will be fulfilled.

THE FOOLISHNESS OF THOSE WHO RIDICULED IT (V. 2)

There is a story of an officer in the trenches during the First World War who was warned about the accuracy of the enemy snipers. Scoffing at the fear of his men, he boldly presented himself in full view of the enemy, crying, 'Don't be ridiculous! Nobody could hit me from this dist—'

Sadly, like the officer who accompanied the king of Israel, there are those who are incredulous when they hear or read the promises of God.

GOD'S UNLIKELY SERVANTS (VV. 3–11)

God sometimes chooses the most unlikely people to fulfil his word. God's act of deliverance began at the very gate where the sceptical officer would meet his judgement. Four lepers, who knew nothing of the prophecy, were about to implement a plan of self-preservation that would make them unwitting instruments in God's greater plan.

Hundreds of years later, another group of men would hatch a plot of self-preservation, seeking to rid themselves of a teacher from Nazareth who threatened their self interest and undermined their position as the great men of Israel—little knowing that this was the culmination of God's great plan of salvation conceived before the foundation of the world! As the saying goes: 'Man proposes, God disposes.'

The actions of the lepers illustrate some of the needs of sinners who seek God's greater deliverance. Firstly, they recognized their hopeless condition (vv. 3–5). A person will not come to Christ for salvation until he or she realizes that there is no other way. Like the leper who came to Jesus, we must fall at his feet and cry, 'Lord, if you are willing, you can make me clean' (Luke 5:12–13).

Secondly, the lepers took hold of God's providence (vv. 6–8). Their hope was that the Syrians would take pity on them and provide for them. But God had gone before them and miraculously scattered his enemies. When they arrived at the Syrian camp they experienced a provision beyond their wildest dreams. So it is for sinners who come to Christ. Fearful of the judgement of God upon their sin, they will simply settle for mercy. What they receive is the fullness of salvation: the riches of God's kingdom, even being made a joint-heir with Christ!

Thirdly, the lepers soon realized that what God had provided was not just for them (vv. 9–11). Whatever their motive for rushing back to the city, they were right in recognizing that 'this day is a day of good news'.

DOUBTS AND FEARS (VV. 12–15)

Of course, there are always doubters. Life teaches us to be sceptical when we are told things that are 'too good to be true'—there is no such thing as a free lunch! The king was suspicious of a Syrian trap, but his fears were soon dispelled when his own men confirmed the lepers' story (vv. 12–15). The gospel seems incredible to the mind of fallen man. The free gift of eternal life flies in the face of life experience and all religious thinking. Where is the trap? Where is the hidden agenda? There isn't one. And when a man or woman tastes and sees that the Lord is good (Psalm 34:8), the message of salvation is confirmed; it is a day of good news.

PROPHECY FULFILLED (VV. 16–20)

God is true to his word. The prophecy of provision was fulfilled to the letter (v. 16). But there had also been a prophecy of judgement (v. 2). What happened to the king's officer? As Alfred Edersheim puts it:

> He took command of the city gate, utterly unconscious of what so soon would befall him. Heedless of the warning, he rushed to his own destruction. Did he ever look up to heaven, remembering his taunting jeer about the windows that might there be opened? Did he see—not a window opened, but a window closed in the heavens above him? Was no friendly voice raised in warning? Probably the details of yesterday's interview with Elisha had already faded from his mind; for the ungodly for a time forget their sins even when swift vengeance is about to overtake them.[1]

For further study ▶

FOR FURTHER STUDY

1. *This chapter reveals human behaviour at its most barbaric. Read Deuteronomy 28:52–57 and compare it with Jeremiah 17:9; Ecclesiastes 9:3; Matthew 15:19; and Mark 7:21–23. What do these passages tell us about our capacity to sin?*
2. *What lessons can we learn from 2 Kings 7:1–20 about the proclamation of the gospel?*

FOR FURTHER STUDY

1. *Identify some of the famine areas of the world and pray for those affected.*
2. *Do you know of any of God's 'unlikely servants'?*

Notes

1. **Edersheim,** *Practical Truths*, p. 261.

10 The promise keeper

2 Kings 8:1–9:37

'There are three things in providence: God's foreknowing, God's determining, and God's directing all things to their periods and events,' said Thomas Watson.[1]

In this passage we see the promises of God fulfilled both in his care and provision for his people and in his judgement upon his enemies.

GOD CARES FOR HIS PEOPLE (8:1–6)

In our Christian walk we are sometimes required to 'Let go and let God'. There are times when we can clearly see a situation developing where action is needed, and that action is the simple step of obedience to the Word of God. There are times, however, when a different kind of obedience is required: a trust in what God says, simply because he says it; a dependence upon God's providential care that takes us beyond our understanding and our own self-reliance. This is the situation that the Shunammite now found herself in. We see the words of Thomas Watson graphically exemplified in her story, and discover some of the ways in which God operates his providential care.

OBEDIENCE TO GOD'S WORD (VV. 1–2)

The woman was told to leave her land. The reason given was that 'the LORD has called for a famine'. The woman simply obeyed. Why? Her confidence in God and his prophet arose out of her recent experience of his provision and powers of restoration. In other words, she had learned to trust God. Elisha had spoken with authority and promised her a son, and God had given her a son. Death had cruelly snatched the son from her, and God had miraculously restored him to her (2 Kings 4:8–37). It is interesting to note that the word 'restore' seems to be a theme running through these first six verses. In the woman's mind, if God had decreed the famine, anything that would be taken from her would be restored just as her son had been.

It is often our past experiences of God's provision and his faithfulness to his word that gives us the faith to trust him for future provision. It has been said that faith is like a muscle: the more we exercise it, the stronger it gets!

DIVINELY ORDERED CIRCUMSTANCES (VV. 3–6)

The identical twins Alec and Eric Bedser were well-known English cricketers during the 1940s and 1950s. When they retired, each was presented with twenty one-pound premium bonds (a kind of lottery) by his grateful county. Thirty-one years later, on the same day, each received a letter informing him that he had won £500. The odds on such a coincidence happening are phenomenal!

Amazing coincidences sometimes occur. But in God's providence there is no such thing as coincidence or luck. Seven years after the famine, the woman returned to reclaim her home and her land from the king. On the very day she came to petition him, the king, intrigued by Elisha, had summoned the prophet's servant Gehazi. Just as the servant was telling the king about the restoration of the woman's son, the mother and son themselves appeared at court! Gehazi, who had been struck with leprosy for his deception of Naaman, was acting as a faithful witness and instrument of God for the woman's provision.

THE ABUNDANCE OF GOD'S PROVISION (V. 6)

The king was not slow in granting the Shunammite's request and even went beyond her immediate plea. She received not only all that she had left behind, but also 'the proceeds of the field from the day that she left the land until now'.

God is gracious, and the experience of his people is of grace upon grace. He has promised abundantly to bless obedience (Malachi 3:10).

THE AGONY OF EVIL (8:7–15)

Just as God predicts and fulfils his promise of provision, so he does likewise with his judgement. God, in his grace and mercy, will often delay that judgement, but it will surely come. Events were now moving to the point where the commission to Elijah—to anoint Hazael, Jehu and Elisha as instruments of his judgement over the house of Ahab—was to be fulfilled (1 Kings 19:15–18). This also marked the end of Elisha's ministry in Israel.

Often when we look at a situation it seems impossible to envisage how God is going to fulfil his promise. Hazael, a trusted official in the Syrian court, was to be anointed king of

Syria, bring judgement on Israel and stamp out Baal worship. But King Ben-Hadad stood in the way. It is not coincidental that the name Hazael means 'God sees'. God knew the wicked heart of Hazael, and the circumstances in which he was going to take the throne of Syria were foreordained. It was now that God revealed this to Elisha.

WHEN PEOPLE ARE DESPERATE THEY OFTEN TURN TO GOD (VV. 7–10)

Ben-Hadad was sick and sent Hazael to Elisha (vv. 7–9). Ben-Hadad's commander, Naaman, had been cleansed of leprosy by the man of God and had returned to Syria with a desire to worship the God of Israel. But Ben-Hadad had no such desire until this sickness came upon him; his own gods were of no use to him now. Many turn to God in time of crisis and discover his grace and mercy. But fallen human nature has a hard heart, and often those who have been blessed do not continue to walk with him. Jesus cleansed ten lepers, but only one returned to thank him (Luke 17:11–19).

WEEPING OVER EVIL (VV. 11–15)

The man of God knew that Ben-Hadad would recover from his illness, but a more sinister scenario had also been revealed to him. Ben-Hadad would recover—but he would die at the hand of Hazael! Elisha had been entrusted with the sure knowledge that this was the beginning of God's judgement upon his own people, and this knowledge broke his heart!

God's servants do not live in a vacuum. The message of God's judgement is to their own kith and kin. Jeremiah wept over his ministry (Jeremiah 9:1); Ezekiel was overwhelmed as he sat among the exiles of his people (Ezekiel 3:15). Jesus,

God's Son, became fully human in order to redeem a people who were under the righteous judgement of God. He came to proclaim that judgement, and also to call people to repent and believe that he was the one who would stand in their place and take that judgement upon himself. But he knew that many would reject him and face their judgement alone. Here was God, fully identified with humanity, feeling the agony of his own people (Luke 19:41–44).

Dale Ralph Davis writes,

> You may think this is not the most spellbinding narrative in the Bible, but it is instructive nonetheless. In one kindness the woman received you should see a kindness that should hearten you; in the truth the king received you should see a responsibility that should alarm you; in the tears the prophet shed you should see a judgement that should sadden you. You have seen here the Lord who revives and slays.[2]

GOD KEEPS HIS PROMISE OF JUDGEMENT (8:16–29)

In his play *An Inspector Calls*, J. B. Priestley gathers the Birling family together for a dinner party in celebration of the engagement of one of the daughters. The meal is interrupted by the mysterious appearance of a police inspector investigating the suicide of a working-class girl who had once been in their employ. Under his interrogation, every member of the family reveals a secret that links him or her with the girl's death. Similarly, God, the writer of history, now brings the characters together for the final scene of his judgement upon the Ahab/Jezebel dynasty!

An alliance was made between the divided kingdoms of Israel and Judah; the kings bore the same name. Like the

Birling family, each had a guilty past. Jehoram (or Joram), king of Israel, the second son of Ahab and Jezebel, had attempted to destroy the Melkart Baal idols (2 Kings 3:1–3), but he had 'persisted in the sins of Jeroboam' (2 Kings 3:3). He was soon to face God's judgement.

Jehoram (or Joram), king of Judah, had married Athaliah, the daughter of Ahab and Jezebel. He had murdered all his brothers as soon as he came to the throne, and had brought the ways of his in-laws into Judah (2 Chronicles 21:1–3). At the same time, Edom and Libnah revolted against the rule of Judah, and Jehoram had led an army against them. A letter from the prophet Elijah had warned him of God's judgement upon his family and predicted the exact circumstances of his death (2 Chronicles 21:12–15). Jehoram died of an intestinal disease after seeing all his family except his youngest son taken into exile, and probably killed, by the Philistines. He was given no honour by the people and not buried in the tombs of the kings (2 Chronicles 21:16–20). The judgement of God was falling!

GOD KEEPS HIS PROMISE OF SALVATION (8:19)

This verse of glorious hope stands in the midst of this terrible act of God's judgement upon sin: 'Yet the LORD would not destroy Judah, for the sake of his servant David, as he promised him to give a lamp to him and his sons forever.' The lamp of God's salvation will never be extinguished.

GOD'S COVENANT WITH DAVID

When your days are over and you rest with your fathers, I will raise up your offspring to succeed you, who will come from your own body, and I will establish his kingdom. He is the one who will build a house for my Name, and I will establish the throne of his kingdom for ever. I will be his father, and he shall be my son. When he does wrong, I will punish him with the rod of men, with floggings inflicted by men. But my love will never be taken away from him, as I took it away from Saul, whom I removed from before you. Your house and your kingdom shall endure for ever before me; your throne shall be established for ever (2 Samuel 7:12–16, NIV).

During his lifetime, David was that lamp, but it continued to burn in his descendants even though there were many attempts to extinguish it. David himself knew that there would be one descendant in whom it would burn with all the brightness of God's glory (Psalm 132:17–18). In the coming of Jesus, the Son of David, God's promise of salvation was fulfilled. He is the inextinguishable Light of God that came into the world (John 1:4–5,9).

JUDGEMENT COMPLETED (9:1–37)

The final character in God's triumvirate of judgement now appeared on the scene, as Elisha gave his final command in his ministry to Israel. Jehu, a member of Ahab's bodyguard, was anointed king over Israel (vv. 1–13).

Under God's providence, God had gathered at Jezreel all those who were awaiting judgement: King Jehoram of Israel, King Ahaziah of Judah, and Jezebel. The first to fall was Jehoram. Severely wounded in a campaign against the Syrians, he had returned to his mother's home to recover. As he tried to escape he was struck down by Jehu's arrow and his body was flung into Naboth's vineyard.

Ahaziah, who had succeeded Jehoram, king of Judah, fled to Beth Haggan, but was soon caught and executed. Because he was the grandson of Jehoshaphat, his body was carried back to Jerusalem for burial.

Finally, Jezebel met her end just as Elijah had predicted (1 Kings 21:1–24).

God's judgement may well have seemed a long time coming. But it was sure to the very end. 'The desire of the wicked shall perish' (Psalm 112:10).

For further study ▶

FOR FURTHER STUDY

1. *The Bible exhorts the reader to 'Trust in the Lord with all your heart' (Proverbs 3:5). The Shunammite did this. Find other examples of this trust in Scripture.*

2. *In 2 Kings 8:19 we read of God's covenant with David. Read the following passages: 2 Samuel 7:12–16; 2 Chronicles 7:17–18; Isaiah 55:3; Jeremiah 33:21; Matthew 1:1; Revelation 3:7; 5:5. What do they teach us about the nature of this covenant?*

FOR FURTHER STUDY

1. *God sees the good heart and the evil heart. What does God see in your heart?*

2. *How can we find hope in the midst of God's judgement? (See 2 Chronicles 7:14; Romans 5:12–21; 2 Corinthians 7:10.)*

Notes

1. Quoted in **I. D. E. Thomas,** *A Puritan Golden Treasury*, (Edinburgh: Banner of Truth, 1977), p. 229.
2. **Davis,** *2 Kings*, p. 136.

11 'Death, where is your sting?'

2 Kings 13:10–25

God may call his servants to work in the spotlight of public recognition for many years or just for a short period of time. Some, like Robert Murray M'Cheyne or Samuel Rutherford, may blaze across the vista of the church like shooting stars, only to burn out at the apex of their ministry. Others, like William Booth, may stay within the public gaze and even be honoured by the nation well into old age.

THE WILDERNESS YEARS (VV. 10–13)

Born in 1878 in Loughor, Wales, Evan Roberts spent the formative years of his life in preparation for what would become a remarkable ministry. At the age of twelve he left school to work in a coal mine along with his father. Twelve years later, now an apprentice blacksmith, Roberts was accepted as a candidate for the Calvanistic Methodist ministry and in 1904 he entered Bible college at Newcastle Emlyn. For many years, Roberts had been praying for revival and by the time he entered college there were indications of a moving of the Holy Spirit in various parts of Wales. Filled with a deep compassion for lost souls, he returned to his home church at Loughor. What followed was a short period of intense meetings, conducted in the blaze of publicity, as revival spread like wildfire across Wales. Sleepless nights, doctrinal confusion and inner struggles soon took their toll on Roberts, and by the spring of 1906 he had fallen into deep depression and he withdrew from the public gaze. Roberts made few further public appearances and died in 1951. Apart from writing his controversial book *War on the Saints*—which he later denounced—only God knows how he spent those forty-five wilderness years away from the public gaze!

Matthew Henry estimated that the period between the anointing of Jehu and the death of Elisha occupied approximately forty-five years. But it is clear that, although we have no record of his ministry during that time, Elisha was not a broken man—far from it! Much had happened in the history of Israel during this period and we can be sure that Elisha was still active in his ministry to the nation and in the schooling of the prophets. Jehoash (Joash) was now on the throne, and it is clear that with his reign nothing had changed among the monarchs of Israel: 'And he did evil in the sight of the LORD. He did not depart from all the sins of Jeroboam the son of Nebat, who made Israel sin, but walked in them' (v. 11).

God's servants never work in obscurity. Even those who are laid aside for long periods of time and can do little more than pray or write letters to encourage fellow servants are under the gaze of their heavenly Father. Earth may have no record of their exploits or of their contribution made to the furtherance of God's kingdom, but heaven will have recorded all that has taken place during those 'wilderness years'.

THE ARROWS OF GOD (VV. 14–25)

GOD'S SERVANTS GET SICK (V. 14)

There are some within the church who teach that it is not God's will that any of his servants should be sick. If a Christian becomes ill, it is a result of unconfessed sin. God's great evangelical prophet Elisha was sick and dying. It would be a brave and foolish man who would attribute his illness to unconfessed sin!

God's servants are not exempt from the effect of the sin of the world. Disease does not pass them by. C. H. Spurgeon suffered intense pain and was laid aside for long periods of time for much of his ministry. William Cowper suffered prolonged bouts of severe depression, yet gave us a legacy of great hymns.

From his sickbed, Elisha exercised a final prophetic act before he drew his last breath. Times of sickness, even our last, may withdraw us from public activity, but they certainly do not withdraw us from usefulness. Robert Murray M'Cheyne recounted the ministry of James Laing, a young man who contracted a fever in his childhood and spent much of his short life in bed. Young James, who had come to know Christ as his Saviour at the age of eleven, was eager to witness to his family and to the young people in his Sabbath school. He spent much time in prayer for them and during the gruelling last three years of his life, took every opportunity to witness to them at his bedside. By the time he died, at the age of fourteen, he had led many of them to Christ.

It is obvious from the text that Elisha was still highly thought of, even by the apostate king of Israel, Jehoash, who was filled with grief at the thought of the prophet's departure. The king's grief was not fuelled by godliness, but by the intense fear that Elisha's death would remove God's protection over his people. His cry, 'O my father, my father, the chariots of Israel and their horsemen!', echoing Elisha's own words at the departure of Elijah, would certainly indicate this. Even the godless receive some crumb of comfort at the presence of the godly!

THE ARROWS FIRED (VV. 14–17)

In the legend of Robin Hood, the hero, being seriously ill, went to his cousin, the prioress at Kirklees, who had great fame for the letting of blood. He was welcomed and his vein opened forthwith. But finding himself locked in, faint and with no means of staunching the flow of blood, Robin suspected treachery. He made a feeble attempt to sound his horn. Fortunately, Little John heard and crashed through the door into his sickroom. From his comrade's arms Robin shot an arrow through the window, saying, 'Bury me where it falls.' And there they buried him, as he wished, with his bow at his side and green turf under his head.

It was not Elisha's intention to be buried where his arrow fell to the ground. His purpose was greater and for the good of the nation he had faithfully served for so long. The arrow that the dying prophet fired was a demonstration of victory over God's enemies. David had declared this in Psalm 64, when, having spoken of the bitter words of the godless against the godly, he went on to say, 'But God shall shoot at them with an arrow. Suddenly they shall be wounded' (v. 7). The shooting of arrows had been the means by which Saul's evil intentions for him were communicated (1 Samuel 20:20–36). King Jehoash now knew for sure that it was not God's intention to allow his people to be taken into captivity; here was the opportunity for him to take hold of God's mighty power and rid God's people of Syrian oppression forever. But the opportunity was lost!

THE ARROWS STRUCK (VV. 18–19,22–25)

People who do not walk with God have no understanding of the ways of God. A channel of God's grace was now fully opened to the king. Elisha's command to strike the ground with the arrows would have made no sense to him. He obeyed out of reverence for the man of God, and possibly with an inkling that this bizarre ritual had some meaning or purpose known to the prophet, but it was mystifying to him. The firing of an arrow signalled God's mighty power—he had already been told that—and all he had to do was shoot as many as he could into the ground, but he held back. If the gospel is hidden, it is hidden from the lost (2 Corinthians 4:3). It makes no sense to fallen man. It is a wholehearted faith that saves a man, and it is a wholehearted faith that takes hold of God's promises. How many have come close to this and been 'almost persuaded', but, like King Jehoash, have held back from full commitment? A temporary blessing followed—in accordance with God's promise, Jehoash defeated the Syrians and recaptured the cities of Israel—but full deliverance was denied.

So there be some who think that hearing the gospel is a little thing. Life, death, and hell, and worlds unknown, may hang upon the preaching and hearing of a sermon. To hear attentively, and not be disturbed in the sermon, may seem a very insignificant thing; and yet upon the catching of the word may result either the attainment of faith or the absence of faith, and so the salvation that comes by faith (C. H. Spurgeon).[1]

THE UNDYING INFLUENCE (VV. 20–21)

Biblical passages are cited to give credibility to 'miracles' associated with relics. The power of Peter's shadow (Acts 5:15) and of Paul's handkerchiefs or aprons (Acts 19:11–12) are frequently quoted. Much is made of the events associated with the burial of Elisha. Those who use this passage in such a way, however, miss the point of its teaching.

To understand the miracle we need to look first at the circumstances in which it took place. With Elisha's death came the lifting of God's hand of protection over Israel. Raiding parties of Moabites soon became a frequent threat to Israel. Disorientated by the appearance of such a band and fearing for their own lives, a funeral party removed the wrong rock and threw the body they were interring into Elisha's tomb. The Israelites did not bury their dead in coffins, but wrapped them in linen cloths and laid them in tombs cut out of the rock. The tomb was then covered with a stone, which could easily be removed. The dead man, who was placed hurriedly in the tomb which had been opened, could therefore easily come into contact with the bones of Elisha. There are a number of lessons we can draw from this passage.

A VERIFICATION OF PROPHECY

This miracle was, in a sense, a continuation of the prophet's ministry to Israel. Judgement would fall upon them, but even so, the God of Israel was a God of the living not the dead. The miracle was intended to stir the king and the people of Israel to continue believing Elisha's prophecies concerning the coming war with the Syrians.

'AND BY FAITH HE STILL SPEAKS, EVEN THOUGH HE IS DEAD'

If the people of Israel walked in the ways of Elisha, they too would know the protecting hand of God's presence, even though his servant was dead. It was not the body of the dead prophet that raised the man to life, but the living God of Israel who had power even over death! We may venerate the lives of godly men and women of previous generations, read their books and marvel at their ministries; but if those who are dead still speak to us (Hebrews 11:4), we do them a disservice and nullify their witness when we look to *them* and not to the God they loved and served.

THE GOD OF RESURRECTION

We see much in the life of Elisha that points us to Christ, and in his death we see not only the miracle of resurrection but also an anticipation of the Saviour's life and ministry in us. Not only was Christ raised from the dead, he *is* the resurrection and the life for all who know him as their Saviour. We do not need to, nor can we, touch his bones, for he has ascended into heaven. The Christian's faith and hope are in the risen Christ (1 Corinthians 15).

Only in eternity will we know fully the debt we owe to the God who revealed himself so wonderfully in the life of this prophet. Krummacher closes his study on the life of Elisha in the following way:

But we must conclude and bid our prophet farewell. When at length we shall walk with him under the palm-trees of Eden, he will explain the miracles and the mysteries of his life to us, more fully and profoundly than we have been able to do, through the troubled vision of earthly manifestation. Till then, let his glorious image, surrounded by the fiery flame of love, continue to live in our hearts, as a radiant testimony what great things the Lord effects in the children of men; and as a lovely star, pointing out to us the direction, which our course must take, if we wish to depart at length in peace.

For further study ▶

FOR FURTHER STUDY

1. *How do the claims of those who believe that Christians should not suffer sickness compare with Elisha's condition and the experiences of Jacob and Paul (see Genesis 48:1–2; 49:29–33; 2 Corinthians 12:7–10)?*
2. *Examine the following biblical examples of how miracles were used to verify the ministry of God's servants: John 6:2,14; Acts 2:22; 15:12; 2 Corinthians 12:12. Should we expect such miraculous verification today? See Luke 16:31; John 20:24–29; 1 Corinthians 1:18–25.*

FOR FURTHER STUDY

1. *How often do we fall short of the blessing that God intends for us because we are not aware of the extent of his promises? How can we become more aware?*
2. *What important lessons can we derive from Elisha's ministry in life and in death?*

Notes

1. **Charles Haddon Spurgeon,** *The Treasury of the Bible*, Grand Rapids: Baker Book House, 1981), vol. 1, p. 877.
2. **F. W. Krummacher,** *The Last Days of Elisha*, (Grand Rapids: Baker Book House, 1981), p. 296.

Further reading

Dale Ralph Davis, *2 Kings: The Power and the Fury* (Fearn, Tain: Christian Focus Publications)

Alfred Edersheim, *Practical Truths from Elisha* (Grand Rapids: Kregel Publications)

F. W. Krummacher, *Elisha: A Prophet for our Times* (Grand Rapids: Kregel Publications)

F. W. Krummacher, *The Last Days of Elisha* (Grand Rapids: Baker Book House)

About Day One:

Day One's threefold commitment:

- To be faithful to the Bible, God's inerrant, infallible Word;
- To be relevant to our modern generation;
- To be excellent in our publication standards.

I continue to be thankful for the publications of Day One. They are biblical; they have sound theology; and they are relative to the issues at hand. The material is condensed and manageable while, at the same time, being complete—a challenging balance to find. We are happy in our ministry to make use of these excellent publications.

JOHN MACARTHUR, PASTOR-TEACHER, GRACE COMMUNITY CHURCH, CALIFORNIA

It a great encouragement to see Day One making such excellent progress. Their publications are always biblical, accessible and attractively produced, with no compromise on quality. Long may their progress continue and increase!

JOHN BLANCHARD, AUTHOR, EVANGELIST AND APOLOGIST

Visit our website for more information and to request a free catalogue of our books.

www.dayone.co.uk

Face2face Samuel— Encountering the king-maker

ROGER ELLSWORTH

128PP, PAPERBACK

ISBN 978–1–84625–039–2

Welcome to the world of dirt roads and oxcarts, cattle and sheep, sandals and robes! Welcome to the world of Samuel—one of the most important men in the history of the nation of Israel. Samuel was a great prophet occupying a unique position in the history of his nation. For a long time, Israel had been ruled by 'judges', but Samuel ushered them into a new era in which they were governed by kings. However, we are not taking this 'face2face' look at Samuel because we are interested in his historical uniqueness but rather because he can help us to know the God who made us and who has a wonderful purpose for all who live for him.

Roger Ellsworth has served as pastor of Immanuel Baptist Church, Benton, Illinois, for eighteen years. He is the author of twenty-seven books, including *Opening up Philippians* and *Opening up Psalms*.

'Roger Ellsworth's book is an extremely relevant and helpful study in the life of Samuel, a much-neglected Old Testament character. It is an extremely practical, pastoral and, most important of all, Christ-exalting-character study at its best and an invaluable addition to a promising series.'

Derek Prime

Face to face Elijah—Encountering Elijah the fiery prophet

SIMON J ROBINSON

80PP, PAPERBACK

ISBN 978–1–84625–011–8

Elijah, the fiery prophet, lived in a time of intense spiritual darkness. People were openly disobeying God's commands, and true worship seemed to have been all but snuffed out. And yet God was still at work! Bringing the power of his word and Spirit into this situation, he used Elijah to break the darkness and to draw people back to himself. This fascinating encounter with Elijah draws out his significance in God's plan and provides us with practical help to live for Christ in the spiritual darkness of the twenty-first century. Each chapter includes questions and points for reflection, making this an ideal book to be used in small groups or for personal study and devotion.

Simon Robinson is the senior minister of Walton Evangelical Church, Chesterfield, England. He has also written several other books, all published by Day One, including *Jesus, the life-changer, Improving your quiet time, Opening up 1 Timothy,* and *God, the Bible and terrorism.* He also preaches and teaches in Asia and the United States. He and his wife, Hazel, have two sons and one grandson.

'With a pastoral and practical touch, Simon Robinson focuses key incidents in the prophet's life and pinpoints helpful lessons to be learned from his life and times.'

John Blanchard

Face to face David volume 1—Encountering the man after God's heart

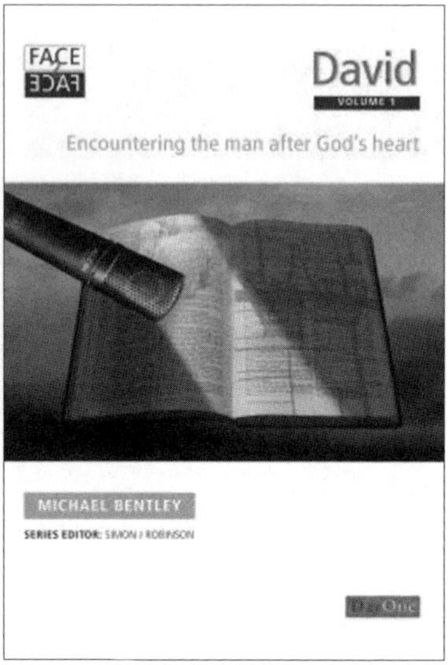

MICHAEL BENTLEY

96PP, PAPERBACK

ISBN 978–1–84625–040–8

Raised in obscurity, young David would not have featured on a list of candidates for the future king of Israel-but God had different ideas! Read, here, about how God's magnificent plan unfolded in the life of this remarkable man and in the lives of those around him.

Michael Bentley worked as a bookshop manager and served in the British army before his call to the ministry. He has a diverse background, which includes broadcasting, teaching Religious Education, and holding pastorates in Surrey, South East London, and Berkshire, while being closely involved with his local community. Now retired, he lives in Bracknell with his wife, Jenny, and has five children and six grandchildren. He is the author of ten books.

'Michael Bentley has an enviable knowledge of the Bible and an admirably simple way of relating its events, and then interweaving the stories with their relevance to our life. Thus, we see how the actions related in the bible can still be appropriate today in the way we live our lives.'

Fran Godfrey, BBC Radio 2 Newsreader/Announcer

Face to face David volume 2—Encountering the king who reigned in power

MICHAEL BENTLEY

144PP, PAPERBACK

ISBN 978–1–84625–015–6

Raised in obscurity, shooting to prominence in the nation of Israel, David became a powerful figure and everyone loved him—well, not quite everyone. Read about his battles, his triumphs, and also his troubles in this engaging, easy-to-use guide.

Michael Bentley worked as a bookshop manager and served in the British army before his call to the ministry. He has a diverse background, which includes broadcasting, teaching Religious Education, and holding pastorates in Surrey, South East London, and Berkshire, while being closely involved with his local community. Now retired, he lives in Bracknell with his wife, Jenny, and has five children and six grandchildren. He is the author of ten books.

'Michael Bentley treats the life of David in a simple, straightforward fashion, never losing sight throughout of the practical significance he has for us, and constantly holding before us David's greater Son, the Lord Jesus. A very good and satisfying book!'

ROGER ELLSWORTH, PASTOR OF IMMANUEL BAPTIST CHURCH, BENTON, ILLINOIS, USA, AND BIBLE COMMENTATOR

'... a book which is full of wisdom ...'

CHRIS PORTER, MINISTER, EASTHAMPSTEAD BAPTIST CHURCH, ENGLAND

Face to face Sennacherib—Encountering Assyria's great and terrifying ruler

CLIVE ANDERSON

96PP, PAPERBACK

ISBN 978–1–84625–076–7

Sennacherib was once a name to send a chill down spines, yet today, relatively few have heard of him, and even fewer know much about him. Lord Byron immortalized one part of his life in a poem, but there was much more to this man than King and fearsome warrior. Coming face to face with him in this book not only reveals a complex and multi-talented man, but also the formidable enemy that the land of Judah, its king Hezekiah and prophet Isaiah were confronted with at a time of national crisis.

Today, many Christians across the world find themselves faced with situations that appear to be beyond their control. How should they react in such circumstances and what help can they expect to receive? This book, while dealing with real history, also focuses on life in the twenty-first century and gives pointers towards being faithful witnesses of Jesus Christ.

Clive Anderson is the pastor of the Butts Church in Alton, Hampshire, and a member of The British Museum Society, The British School of Archaeology in Iraq, and The Egyptian Exploration Society, and leads tours to the Middle East and Egypt and around the British Museum. He is the author of *Opening up Nahum*, *Opening up 2 Peter*, *Travel with Spurgeon*, *Gunpowder, Treason and Plot*, and has co-authored with Brian Edwards

Through the British Museum with the Bible, all published by Day One. Clive had spoken in the USA, Europe, and in the Far East, and is also a frequent broadcaster on local radio. He and his wife, Amanda, have one son.

'Clive Anderson brings ancient history to life. Out of the stony slabs of antiquity, Sennacherib emerges, flesh and blood. Using biblical sources and drawing on his extensive knowledge of archaeology and ancient history, Clive Anderson gives the reader a fascinating insight into the life and times of this notorious Assyrian king—enriching and sharpening our understanding of the biblical text. This book is a must for preachers and teachers and an invaluable aid to Bible study. It is easily accessible scholarship—providing accurate background knowledge, sound biblical exposition and searching application.'

Rev. Dr Jim Winter, Pastor, Horsell Evangelical Church, and author of several books

'Clive Anderson brings two great passions to bear in the writing of this book. The first is that by filling in the blanks of our map of Old Testament history the key points which God highlights would be better seen and understood by God's people. The second is that from a clearer understanding of God's dealings with his people would flow a clearer desire to walk in God's ways. Both passions are plain to see throughout this book and applied with insight and wisdom by a very knowledgeable and passionate writer.'

Chris Hughes, Pastor of Bishopstoke Evangelical Church, Hampshire, England

'A gem of a book'

Rev. Dr Iain D Campbell